CONTENTS

WELCOME TO NORTHSTAR
SECOND EDITION

NorthStar, now in a new edition, motivates students to succeed in their **academic** as well as **personal** language goals.

For each of the five levels, the two strands—*Reading and Writing* and *Listening and Speaking*—provide a fully integrated approach for students and teachers.

WHAT IS SPECIAL ABOUT THE NEW EDITION?

NEW THEMES

New themes and **updated content**—presented in a **variety of genres**, including literature and lectures, and in **authentic reading and listening selections**—challenge students intellectually.

ACADEMIC SKILLS

More purposeful **integration of critical thinking** and an enhanced focus on **academic skills** such as inferencing, synthesizing, note taking, and test taking help students develop strategies for **success** in the **classroom** and on **standardized tests.** A culminating **productive task** galvanizes content, language, and **critical thinking skills**.

➤ In the *Reading and Writing* strand, a new, **fully integrated writing section** leads students through the **writing process** with engaging writing assignments focusing on various rhetorical modes.

➤ In the *Listening and Speaking* strand, a **structured approach** gives students opportunities for **more extended and creative oral practice**, for example, presentations, simulations, debates, case studies, and public service announcements.

NEW DESIGN

Full **color pages** with more **photos, illustrations, and graphic organizers** foster student engagement and make the content and activities come alive.

MyNorthStarLab

MyNorthStarLab, an easy-to-use **online learning and assessment program**, offers:

➤ Unlimited access to reading and listening selections and DVD segments.

➤ Focused test preparation to help students succeed on international exams such as TOEFL® and IELTS®. Pre- and post-unit assessments improve results by providing individualized instruction, instant feedback, and personalized study plans.

➤ Original activities that support and extend the *NorthStar* program. These include pronunciation practice using voice recording tools, and activities to build note taking skills and academic vocabulary.

➤ Tools that save time. These include a flexible gradebook and authoring features that give teachers control of content and help them track student progress.

THE NORTHSTAR APPROACH

The *NorthStar* series is based on **current research in language acquisition** and on the **experiences of teachers and curriculum designers**. Five principles guide the *NorthStar* approach.

PRINCIPLES

1 **The more profoundly students are stimulated intellectually and emotionally, the more language they will use and retain.**

The thematic organization of *NorthStar* promotes intellectual and emotional stimulation. The 50 sophisticated themes in *NorthStar* present intriguing topics such as recycled fashion, restorative justice, personal carbon footprints, and microfinance. The authentic content engages students, links them to language use outside of the classroom, and encourages personal expression and critical thinking.

2 **Students can learn both the form and content of the language.**

Grammar, vocabulary, and culture are inextricably woven into the units, providing students with systematic and multiple exposures to language forms in a variety of contexts. As the theme is developed, students can express complex thoughts using a higher level of language.

3 **Successful students are active learners.**

Tasks are designed to be creative, active, and varied. Topics are interesting and up-to-date. Together these tasks and topics (1) allow teachers to bring the outside world into the classroom and (2) motivate students to apply their classroom learning in the outside world.

4 **Students need feedback.**

This feedback comes naturally when students work together practicing language and participating in open-ended opinion and inference tasks. Whole class activities invite teachers' feedback on the spot or via audio/video recordings or notes. The innovative new MyNorthStarLab gives students immediate feedback as they complete computer-graded language activities online; it also gives students the opportunity to submit writing or speaking assignments electronically to their instructor for feedback later.

5 **The quality of relationships in the language classroom is important because students are asked to express themselves on issues and ideas.**

The information and activities in *NorthStar* promote genuine interaction, acceptance of differences, and authentic communication. By building skills and exploring ideas, the exercises help students participate in discussions and write essays of an increasingly complex and sophisticated nature.

THE NORTHSTAR UNIT

① FOCUS ON THE TOPIC

This section introduces students to the unifying theme
of the reading selections.

> **PREDICT** and **SHARE INFORMATION** foster interest in the unit topic and help
> students develop a personal connection to it.
>
> **BACKGROUND AND VOCABULARY** activities provide students with tools for
> understanding the first reading selection. Later in the unit, students review
> this vocabulary and learn related idioms, collocations, and word forms. This
> helps them explore content and expand their written and spoken language.

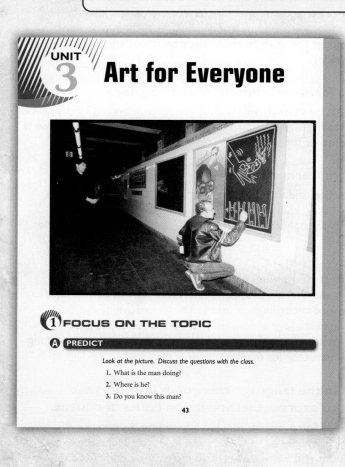

UNIT 3 — Art for Everyone

① FOCUS ON THE TOPIC

Ⓐ PREDICT

Look at the picture. Discuss the questions with the class.

1. What is the man doing?
2. Where is he?
3. Do you know this man?

43

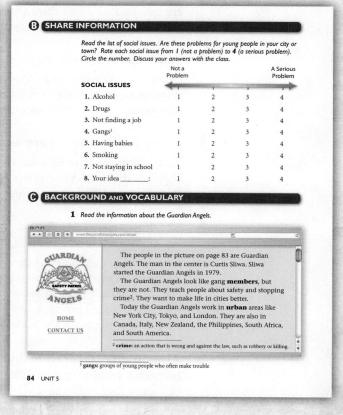

Ⓑ SHARE INFORMATION

Read the list of social issues. Are these problems for young people in your city or town? Rate each social issue from 1 (not a problem) to 4 (a serious problem). Circle the number. Discuss your answers with the class.

SOCIAL ISSUES	Not a Problem			A Serious Problem
1. Alcohol	1	2	3	4
2. Drugs	1	2	3	4
3. Not finding a job	1	2	3	4
4. Gangs[1]	1	2	3	4
5. Having babies	1	2	3	4
6. Smoking	1	2	3	4
7. Not staying in school	1	2	3	4
8. Your idea _____:	1	2	3	4

Ⓒ BACKGROUND AND VOCABULARY

1 *Read the information about the Guardian Angels.*

www.theguardianangels.com/about

GUARDIAN ANGELS
SAFETY PATROL

HOME
CONTACT US

The people in the picture on page 83 are Guardian
Angels. The man in the center is Curtis Sliwa. Sliwa
started the Guardian Angels in 1979.

The Guardian Angels look like gang **members**, but
they are not. They teach people about safety and stopping
crime[2]. They want to make life in cities better.

Today the Guardian Angels work in **urban** areas like
New York City, Tokyo, and London. They are also in
Canada, Italy, New Zealand, the Philippines, South Africa,
and South America.

[2] **crime:** an action that is wrong and against the law, such as robbery or killing.

[1] **gangs:** groups of young people who often make trouble

84 UNIT 5

② FOCUS ON READING

This section focuses on understanding two contrasting reading selections.

READING ONE is a literary selection, academic article, news piece, blog, or other genre that addresses the unit topic. In levels 1 to 3, readings are based on authentic materials. In levels 4 and 5, all the readings are authentic.

READ FOR MAIN IDEAS and **READ FOR DETAILS** are comprehension activities that lead students to an understanding and appreciation of the first selection.

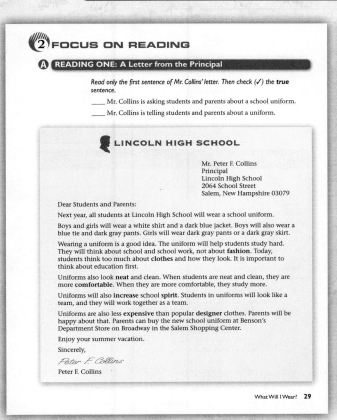

② FOCUS ON READING

Ⓐ READING ONE: A Letter from the Principal

Read only the first sentence of Mr. Collins' letter. Then check (✓) the **true** *sentence.*

____ Mr. Collins is asking students and parents about a school uniform.

____ Mr. Collins is telling students and parents about a uniform.

LINCOLN HIGH SCHOOL

Mr. Peter F. Collins
Principal
Lincoln High School
2064 School Street
Salem, New Hampshire 03079

Dear Students and Parents:

Next year, all students at Lincoln High School will wear a school uniform.

Boys and girls will wear a white shirt and a dark blue jacket. Boys will also wear a blue tie and dark gray pants. Girls will wear dark gray pants or a dark gray skirt.

Wearing a uniform is a good idea. The uniform will help students study hard. They will think about school and school work, not about **fashion**. Today, students think too much about **clothes** and how they look. It is important to think about education first.

Uniforms also look **neat** and clean. When students are neat and clean, they are more **comfortable**. When they are more comfortable, they study more.

Uniforms will also **increase** school **spirit**. Students in uniforms will look like a team, and they will work together as a team.

Uniforms are also less **expensive** than popular **designer** clothes. Parents will be happy about that. Parents can buy the new school uniform at Benson's Department Store on Broadway in the Salem Shopping Center.

Enjoy your summer vacation.

Sincerely,

Peter F. Collins

Peter F. Collins

What Will I Wear? **29**

◖ READ FOR MAIN IDEAS

Read each pair of sentences. Check (✓) the sentence that is true.

1. ____ **a.** Blockbuster is in danger of going out of business.
   ✓ **b.** Captain Video is in danger of going out of business.

2. ____ **a.** Small, locally-owned stores are closing in Stamford.
   ____ **b.** Large chain stores are closing in Stamford.

3. ____ **a.** Mr. Woodroof wants the customers to support the chain stores.
   ____ **b.** Mr. Woodroof wants the customers to support the smaller stores.

4. ____ **a.** Mr. Woodroof is afraid that life in his town is changing.
   ____ **b.** Mr. Woodroof is happy that life in his town is changing.

◖ READ FOR DETAILS

Read each sentence. Circle the correct answer to complete each sentence.

1. Borders is the name of a large ____ chain.
   a. bookstore   **c.** electronics store
   b. drugstore   **d.** video store

2. Captain Video is trying to compete with ____.
   a. video stores   **c.** drugstores
   b. bookstores   **d.** coffee bars

3. Captain Video has more ____ than other video stores in Stamford.
   a. customers   **c.** movies
   b. employees   **d.** video games

4. Captain Video's customers are ____.
   a. changing   **c.** loyal
   b. friendly   **d.** personal

(continued on next page)

Going Out of Business? **113**

Following this comprehension section, the **MAKE INFERENCES** activity prompts students to "read between the lines," move beyond the literal meaning, exercise critical thinking skills, and understand the text on a more academic level. Students follow up with pair or group work to discuss topics in the **EXPRESS OPINIONS** section.

READING TWO offers another perspective on the topic and usually belongs to another genre. Again, in levels 1 to 3, the readings are based on authentic materials, and in levels 4 and 5, they are authentic. This second reading is followed by an activity that challenges students to question ideas they formed about the first reading, and to use appropriate language skills to analyze and explain their ideas.

INTEGRATE READINGS ONE AND TWO presents culminating activities. Students are challenged to take what they have learned, organize the information, and synthesize it in a meaningful way. Students practice skills that are essential for success in authentic academic settings and on standardized tests.

B **READING TWO: Bram Tarek**

1 *Read the imaginary interview with Bram Tarek.*

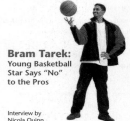

Bram Tarek:
Young Basketball
Star Says "No"
to the Pros

Interview by
Nicola Quinn

You probably don't know Bram Tarek—not yet. But basketball coaches know him, and they think he has a lot of talent. He is a college basketball star. At 18 years old and after graduating from high school, Bram Tarek is now old enough to join a professional basketball team, but the NBA[1] will have to wait. Tarek wants to graduate from college first.

NQ: Bram, everyone expected you to join the NBA this year. Why did you decide to finish college first?
BT: Well, I planned to join the NBA as soon as I was old enough. But then I met

older basketball players. They said I should stay in college.
NQ: Who did you talk to?
BT: Several basketball players. But Kareem Abdul-Jabbar probably helped me the most. He is my biggest basketball hero. He's the greatest. But, in his day, all players had to go to college before joining the NBA. Today it's different. He said college helped the players to become more mature—intellectually and physically.
NQ: But what about the money? How can you say "no" to all that money?
BT: Oh, that was really hard! On the wall in my bedroom, I had photos of all the beautiful cars I wanted to buy!
NQ: So, what happened?
BT: Kareem helped a lot. He really taught me that money is not #1. The important things in life are family, education, and health. And I still have a lot to learn.
NQ: What exactly do you need to learn?
BT: I need to learn more about working with other people—especially with people I don't agree with. I want to be a leader like Kareem. Thirty years from now, I want people to say "Bram Tarek was—or is—a great athlete, a great leader, and a good person," not "Bram Tarek was a great athlete with a lot of expensive cars when he was 18."

[1] **NBA:** National Basketball Association. All professional basketball teams in the U.S. are in the NBA.

C **INTEGRATE READINGS ONE AND TWO**

STEP 1: Organize

Think about New York's problems in Reading Two and the solutions in Reading One. Which solutions might work for each problem? Write the solutions from the box in the chart. More than one answer is possible.

bike lanes	helicopter	sky train	tunnel under city
Deduct-a-Ride	online traffic map	traffic tax	

TRAFFIC PROBLEMS IN NEW YORK CITY	POSSIBLE SOLUTIONS
Trucks	
Poor conditions of roads and bridges	
Streets not safe for pedestrians	
Streets not safe for bicyclists	
Slow buses	
Pollution, including noise	

STEP 2: Synthesize

1 *Work with a partner. One student is Rafael Torres, and the other the mayor of New York. Complete the interview between Torres (T) and the mayor (M). Use the information from the readings. Do not give your own opinion.*

T: Mr. Mayor, as you know, there are serious traffic problems in this city. I have data to show you.

M: Yes, I know. What did the poll say?

T: Well, one big problem is . . .

M: OK, to solve that problem I want to . . .

2 *Change roles and repeat Exercise 1 with a different problem and solution.*

3 *Present one of your conversations to the class.*

---

③ FOCUS ON WRITING

This section emphasizes development of productive skills for writing. It includes sections on vocabulary, grammar, and the writing process.

> The **VOCABULARY** section leads students from reviewing the unit vocabulary, to practicing and expanding their use of it, and then working with it—using it creatively in both this section and in the final writing task.
>
> Students learn useful structures for writing in the **GRAMMAR** section, which offers a concise presentation and targeted practice. Vocabulary items are recycled here, providing multiple exposures leading to mastery. For additional practice with the grammar presented, students and teachers can consult the GRAMMAR BOOK REFERENCES at the end of the book for corresponding material in the *Focus on Grammar* and Azar series.

---

③ FOCUS ON WRITING

Ⓐ VOCABULARY

◀ REVIEW

Read the paragraph. Then fill in the blanks with words from the box.

advice	laughed	quotes
chat	meet	safe
community	peace	users
~~goal~~	personal	volunteers

At 16, Bronwyn Polson's __goal__ (1.) was to do something good for her _____ (2.) and for the world. Bronwyn called newspapers and social service organizations, but they just _____ (3.). They said she was too young to help. So, she started a website called The Friendship Page. She believes in "_____ (4.) through friendship." On The Friendship Page people _____ (5.) new friends. They can _____ (6.) about important things. It has _____ (7.) for people with friendship problems. The _____ (8.) page is the most popular part.

_____ (9.) help Bronwyn. They want The Friendship Page to be _____ (10.) for everyone. _____ (11.) do not give important _____ (12.) information. The Friendship Page is a lot of work, but Bronwyn enjoys it very much.

Ⓑ GRAMMAR: Pronouns and Possessive Adjectives

1 *Read the paragraph. Look at the underlined words. Draw an arrow from each underlined word to the noun it refers to. Then answer the questions.*

What Do Urban Angels Do?

Urban Angels have many activities after school and on Saturdays. They go on trips to local museums and to other places outside the city. They also visit businesses to learn about different jobs. Most important, Urban Angels help out in their community. At "park clean-ups" they go to city parks and make them beautiful again.

1. Which underlined word is a subject?
2. Which underlined word is an object?
3. Which underlined word shows possession?

PRONOUNS AND POSSESSIVE ADJECTIVES	
A **pronoun** is a word that takes the place of a noun. Pronouns are useful when you don't want to repeat a noun in a sentence.	[subject] **Urban Angels** have many activities.
1. **Subject pronouns** take the place of the subject in a sentence. Subject pronouns include: *I, you, he, she, it, we,* and *they*.	[subject pronoun] **They** go on trips to local museums. **You** can become an Urban Angel.
2. **Object pronouns** take the place of an object. Objects usually come after the verb. Object pronouns also come after prepositions like *for, to,* and *from*. Object pronouns include: *me, you, him, her, it, us,* and *them*.	[object] Urban Angels like to help **people**. [object pronoun] Urban Angels teach **them** about safety. The Urban Angels program needs **support**. New York City helps pay for **it**.
3. **Possessive adjectives** are like pronouns. They show possession or ownership. They always come before a noun. Possessive adjectives include: *my, your, his, her, its, our,* and *their*.	Urban Angels help out in **their** community. **My** goal is to be a fashion designer. Kelly isn't an Urban Angel, but **her** friend is.

The **WRITING** section of each unit leads students through the writing process and presents a challenging and imaginative writing task that directs students to integrate the content, vocabulary, and grammar from the unit.

- Students practice a short **pre-writing strategy**, such as freewriting, clustering, brainstorming, interviewing, listing, making a chart or diagram, categorizing, or classifying.

- Then students organize their ideas and write, using a **specific structural or rhetorical pattern** that fits the subject at hand.

- Students then learn **revising techniques** within a sentence-level or paragraph-level activity to help them move towards **coherence and unity** in their writing.

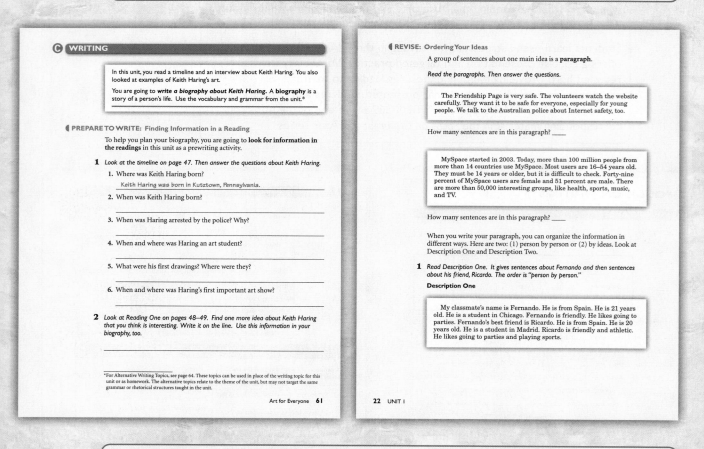

In the final phase of the writing process, students **edit** their work with the help of a **checklist** that focuses on mechanics, completeness, enhancing style, and incorporating the vocabulary and grammar from the unit.

ALTERNATIVE WRITING TOPICS are provided at the end of the unit. They can be used as *alternatives* to the final writing task, or as *additional* assignments. RESEARCH TOPICS tied to the theme of the unit are organized in a special section at the back of the book.

COMPONENTS

TEACHER'S MANUAL WITH ACHIEVEMENT TESTS

Each level and strand of *NorthStar* has an accompanying Teacher's Manual with step-by-step **teaching suggestions**, including unique guidance for using *NorthStar* in secondary classes. The manuals include time guidelines, expansion activities, and techniques and instructions for using MyNorthStarLab. Also included are reproducible unit-by-unit achievement **tests** of **receptive** and **productive** skills, **answer keys** to both the student book and tests, and a unit-by-unit **vocabulary** list.

EXAMVIEW

NorthStar ExamView is a stand-alone CD-ROM that allows teachers to **create and customize** their own *NorthStar* tests.

DVD

The *NorthStar* DVD has **engaging, authentic video clips**, including animation, documentaries, interviews, and biographies, that correspond to the themes in *NorthStar*. Each theme contains a three- to five-minute segment that can be used with either the *Reading and Writing* strand or the *Listening and Speaking* strand. The video clips can also be viewed in MyNorthStarLab.

COMPANION WEBSITE

The companion website, www.longman.com/northstar, includes resources for teachers, such as the **scope and sequence**, **correlations** to other Longman products and to state standards, and **podcasts** from the *NorthStar* authors and series editors.

MyNorthStarLab

PEARSON LONGMAN
mynorthstarlab | AVAILABLE WITH the new edition of *NORTHSTAR*

NorthStar is now available with **MyNorthStarLab**—an easy-to-use **online** program **for students and teachers** that saves time and improves results.

➤ **STUDENTS** receive **personalized instruction** and **practice** in all four skills. Audio, video, and test preparation are all in **one** place—available **anywhere, anytime**.

➤ **TEACHERS** can take advantage of many resources including online **assessments**, a flexible **gradebook**, and **tools for monitoring student progress**.

CHECK IT OUT! GO TO www.mynorthstarlab.com FOR A PREVIEW!

TURN THE PAGE TO SEE KEY FEATURES OF **MyNorthStarLab**.

MYNORTHSTARLAB

MyNorthStarLab supports students with **individualized instruction**, **feedback**, and **extra help**. A wide array of resources, including a flexible **gradebook**, helps teachers manage student progress.

The MyNorthStarLab **WELCOME** page **organizes assignments and grades**, and **facilitates communication** between students and teachers.

For each unit, MyNorthStarLab provides a **READINESS CHECK**.

➤ Activities **assess** student knowledge **before** beginning the unit and **follow up** with individualized instruction.

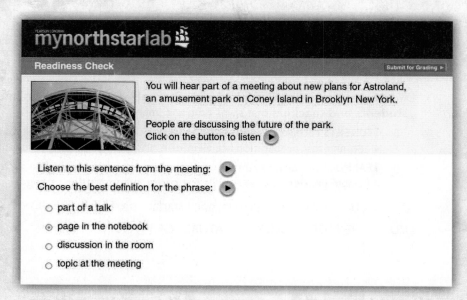

Student book material and **new** practice activities are available to students online.

➤ Students benefit from virtually unlimited **practice anywhere, anytime**.

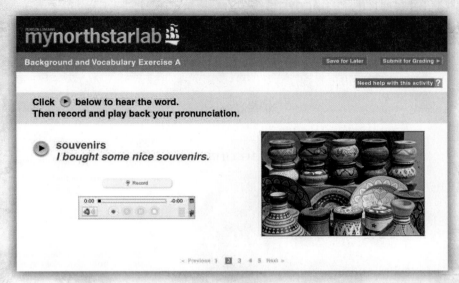

Interaction with **Internet** and **video** materials will:

➤ Expand students' knowledge of the topic.

➤ Help students practice new vocabulary and grammar.

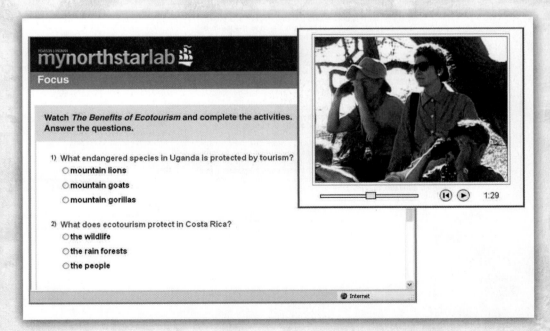

INTEGRATED SKILL ACTIVITIES in MyNorthStarLab challenge students to bring together the **language skills** and **critical thinking skills** that they have practiced throughout the unit.

Integrated Task - Read, Listen, Write   Submit for Grading ▶

THE ADVENTURE OF A LIFETIME

We at the Antarctic Travel Society <u>encourage</u> you to consider an excited guided tour of Antarctica for your next vacation.

The Antarctic Travel society carefully plans and operates tours of the Antarctic by ship. There are three trips per day leaving from <u>ports</u> in South America and Australia. Each ship carries only about 100 passengers at a time. Tours run from November through March to the ice-free areas along the coast of Antarctica.

In addition to touring the coast, our ships stop for on-land visits, which generally last for about three hours. Activities include guided sightseeing, mountain climbing, camping, <u>kayaking</u>, and <u>scuba diving</u>. For a longer stay, camping trips can also be arranged.

Our tours will give you an opportunity to experience the richness of Antarctica, including its wildlife, history, active research stations, and, most of all, its natural beauty.

Tours are <u>supervised</u> by the ship's staff. The staff generally includes <u>experts</u> in animal and sea life and other Antarctica specialists. There is generally one staff member for every 10 to 20 passengers. Theses trained and responsible individuals will help to make your visit to Antarctica safe, educational, and <u>unforgettable</u>.

READ, LISTEN AND WRITE ABOUT TOURISM IN ANTARCTICA
Read.
Read the text. Then answer the question.

According to the text, how can tourism benefit the Antartic?

▶ **Listen.**
Click on the Play button and listen to the passage.
Use the outline to take notes as you listen.

Main idea:

Seven things that scientists study:

The effects of tourism:

Write.
Write about the potential and risks in Antarctica.
Follow the steps to prepare.

Step 1
 • Review the text and your outline from the listening task.
 • Write notes about the benefits and risks of tourism.

Step 2
Write for 20 minutes. Leave 5 minutes to edit your work.

The MyNorthStarLab **ASSESSMENT** tools allow instructors to customize and deliver achievement tests online.

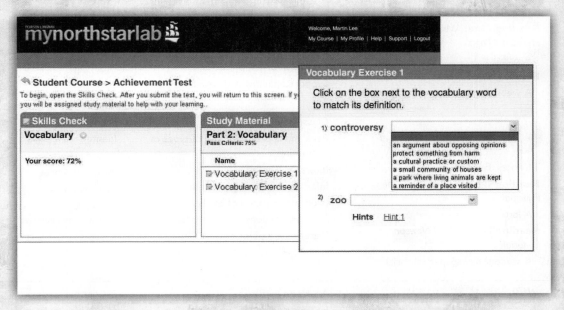

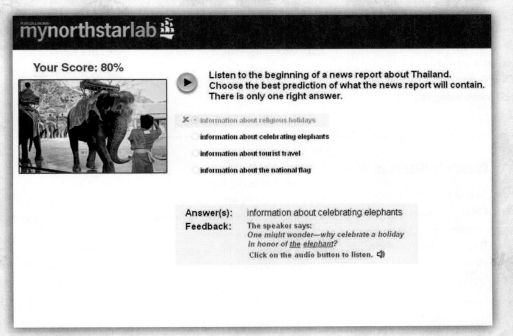

SCOPE AND SEQUENCE

UNIT	CRITICAL THINKING	READING

1 **The Friendship Page**
 	
Theme: Friendship
Reading One: *Welcome to the Friendship Page*
   A website
Reading Two: *Welcome to MySpace*
   A website
	Analyze a picture
	Evaluate and compare Internet use
	Analyze statistical information
	Infer word meaning from context
	Infer information not explicit in the text
	Hypothesize another's point of view
	Classify information
	Support opinions with reasons
		Predict content
		Identify main ideas
		Read for details
		Make inferences
		Express opinions
		Organize and synthesize information from the readings

2 **What Will I Wear?**
 	
Theme: Fashion
Reading One: *A Letter from the Principal*
   A letter to students and parents
Reading Two: *School Newspaper Editorial*
   A student newspaper editorial
	Classify clothing
	Rank the appropriateness of types of clothing
	Interpret a graph
	Infer word meaning from context
	Infer information not explicit in the text
	Support opinions with reasons
	Determine a point of view
		Predict content
		Identify main ideas
		Read for details
		Make inferences
		Express opinions
		Organize and synthesize information from the readings

3 **Art for Everyone**
 	
Theme: The Arts
Reading One: *Art for Everyone*
   A magazine interview
Reading Two: *Look at Haring's Art*
   A descriptive paragraph
	Analyze a picture
	Interpret paintings
	Infer word meaning from context
	Infer information not explicit in the text
	Categorize information
		Predict content
		Identify main ideas
		Read for details
		Make inferences
		Read a timeline
		Correct false statements
		Express opinions
		Organize and synthesize information from the readings

4 **What's It Worth to You?**
 	
Theme: Special Possessions
Reading One: *My Secret*
   A sports column
Reading Two: *Be a Smart Collector*
   A list of rules
	Interpret an illustration
	Discuss possessions
	Infer word meaning from context
	Support opinions with reasons
	Infer information not explicit in the text
	Categorize information
	Relate information in the unit to personal experiences
		Predict content
		Identify main ideas
		Read for details
		Make inferences
		Match examples to information in the reading
		Express opinions
		Organize and synthesize information from the readings

WRITING	VOCABULARY	GRAMMAR
Write answers to questions Use an interview as a pre-writing tool Construct complete sentences Order ideas Write a paragraph about a classmate	Use context clues to find meaning Define words Use vocabulary for greetings	Questions with *be* and *have*
Complete a role play Complete sentences Answer questions Brainstorm ideas for writing Order descriptive adjectives Write an opinion letter	Use context clues to find meaning Define words Classify vocabulary	The future with *will*
Complete sentences Complete a crossword puzzle Find information in the reading Give events in time order Use commas in dates and names of places Write a biography	Use context clues to find meaning Define words Classify vocabulary by part of speech	Simple past of *be* and *have*
Complete a short paragraph Ask questions Stay on topic Write a paragraph about a special possession or collection	Use context clues to find meaning Define words Find word associations Classify vocabulary	The simple present

SCOPE AND SEQUENCE

UNIT	CRITICAL THINKING	READING

5 Strength in Numbers
 	
Theme: Strength in Numbers
Reading One: *Urban Angels*
  An informational brochure
Reading Two: *Two Real Angels*
  An informational brochure
	Analyze a picture
	Rate social issues in your hometown
	Infer word meaning from context
	Infer information not explicit in the text
	Support opinions with reasons
	Categorize information
		Predict content
		Identify main ideas
		Read for details
		Make inferences
		Express opinions
		Read a chart
		Organize and synthesize information
		  from the readings

6 Going Out of Business?
 	
Theme: Business
Reading One: *The Death of the Family-Owned Video Store?*
  A newsletter article
Reading Two: *About Blockbuster Total Access™*
  Information about an online service
	Analyze a picture
	Activate prior knowledge
	Categorize stores in your neighborhood
	Infer word meaning from context
	Support opinions with reasons
	Analyze an advertisement
	Infer information not explicit in the text
	Identify advantages and disadvantages
		Read an advertisement
		Predict content
		Identify main ideas
		Read for details
		Make inferences
		Express opinions
		Organize and synthesize information
		  from the readings

7 Flying High and Low
 	
Theme: Famous People
Reading One: *Lindbergh Did It!*
  A newspaper article
Reading Two: *Timeline of Lindbergh's Life*
  A timeline
	Describe an illustration
	Classify information
	Support answers with information from the text
	Relate information from the unit to personal experiences
	Support inferences
	Hypothesize another's point of view
		Predict content
		Identify main ideas
		Read for details
		Make inferences
		Read a timeline
		Express opinions
		Organize and synthesize information
		  from the readings

WRITING	VOCABULARY	GRAMMAR
Complete sentences Complete a letter Make a list Give examples to support opinions Write a letter to the editor	Use context clues to find meaning Define words Use idiomatic expressions	Pronouns and possessive adjectives
Write questions and answers Write a descriptive paragraph about a business Draw a map Use space order Write a paragraph about a place	Define words Use context clues to find meaning Classify vocabulary	*There is / There are*
Write sentences Complete a diary Make a timeline Write an autobiography Use time order words Write a paragraph about a trip	Define words Use context clues to find meaning Identify synonyms	The simple past

SCOPE AND SEQUENCE

UNIT	CRITICAL THINKING	READING
8 **Are We There Yet?** **Theme:** Driving Problems **Reading One:** *Looking for Traffic Solutions* A memo **Reading Two:** *New Yorkers Talk Traffic, Mayor in the Slow Lane* A newspaper article	Interpret a picture Conduct a survey Compare traffic stories Infer word meaning from context Infer information not explicit in the text Hypothesize another's point of view Evaluate solutions to a problem Support opinions with reasons Identify and compare advantages and disadvantages	Predict content Identify main ideas Read for details Make inferences Express opinions Organize and synthesize information from the readings
9 **Full House** **Theme:** Family **Reading One:** *Full House* A newspaper article **Reading Two:** *The Dionne Quintuplets* A letter	Analyze a picture Compare families Infer word meaning from context Analyze a chart Infer information not explicit in the text Discuss the pros and cons of big families Support opinions with reasons Categorize information	Predict content Read a chart Identify main ideas Read for details Make inferences Express opinions Organize and synthesize information from the readings
10 **How Young Is Too Young?** **Theme:** Sports **Reading One:** *Ready Freddy?* A newspaper article **Reading Two:** *Bram Tarek* An interview	Interpret a picture Compare sports preferences Discuss the benefits and drawbacks of being a professional athlete Infer word meaning from context Infer information not explicit in the text Support opinions with reasons Categorize information Hypothesize another's point of view Express agreement and disagreement	Predict content Identify main ideas Read for details Make inferences Express opinions Organize and synthesize information from the readings

WRITING	VOCABULARY	GRAMMAR
Complete a conversation Write questions and answers Make a chart Compare and contrast Put reasons in order Write a comparison and contrast paragraph about the best way to get to school or work	Define words Use context clues to find meaning	Comparative adjectives
Write answers to questions Complete a letter Interview classmates Write follow-up questions Write a concluding sentence Write an opinion paragraph	Define words Use context clues to find meaning	*Should*
Complete an interview Complete sentences Write a dialogue based on pictures Brainstorm Give strong advice Write a response giving advice	Define words Use context clues to find meaning Use idiomatic expressions	*Very, too,* and *enough*

ACKNOWLEDGMENTS

My sincere thanks and appreciation to Debbie Sistino, Carol Numrich, and Dana Klinek, whose support and guidance made writing this text an enjoyable learning experience.

Also thanks to fellow *NorthStar* authors Polly Merdinger, Natasha Haugnes, and Laurie Barton for sharing their ideas.

I also very much appreciate the valuable contributions of Linda Butler, Kam Chan, Ariel Clemons, Sofia DiGiallonardo, Bronwyn Polson, Edwin Ramoran, and Ellen Sullivan. Many thanks to you all.

John Beaumont

Reviewers

For the comments and insights they graciously offered to help shape the direction of the new edition of *NorthStar*, the publisher would like to thank the following reviewers and institutions.

Gail August, Hostos Community College; **Anne Bachmann**, Clackamas Community College; **Aegina Barnes**, York College, CUNY; **Dr. Sabri Bebawi**, San Jose Community College; **Kristina Beckman**, John Jay College; **Jeff Bellucci**, Kaplan Boston; **Nathan Blesse**, Human International Academy; **Alan Brandman**, Queens College; **Laila Cadavona-Dellapasqua**, Kaplan; **Amy Cain**, Kaplan; **Nigel Caplan**, Michigan State University; **Alzira Carvalho**, Human International Academy, San Diego; **Chao-Hsun (Richard) Cheng**, Wenzao Ursuline College of Languages; **Mu-hua (Yolanda) Chi**, Wenzao Ursuline College of Languages; **Liane Cismowski**, Olympic High School; **Shauna Croft**, MESLS; **Misty Crooks**, Kaplan; **Amanda De Loera**, Kaplan English Programs; **Jennifer Dobbins**, New England School of English; **Luis Dominguez**, Angloamericano; **Luydmila Drgaushanskaya**, ASA College; **Dilip Dutt**, Roxbury Community College; **Christie Evenson**, Chung Dahm Institute; **Patricia Frenz-Belkin**, Hostos Community College, CUNY; **Christiane Galvani**, Texas Southern University; **Joanna Ghosh**, University of Pennsylvania; **Cristina Gomes**, Kaplan Test Prep; **Kristen Grinager**, Lincoln High School; **Janet Harclerode**, Santa Monica College; **Carrell Harden**, HCCS, Gulfton Campus; **Connie Harney**, Antelope Valley College; **Ann Hilborn**, ESL Consultant in Houston; **Barbara Hockman**, City College of San Francisco; **Margaret Hodgson**, NorQuest College; **Paul Hong**, Chung Dahm Institute; **Wonki Hong**, Chung Dahm Institute; **John House**, Iowa State University; **Polly Howlett**, Saint Michael's College; **Arthur Hui**, Fullerton College; **Nina Ito**, CSU, Long Beach; **Scott Jenison**, Antelope Valley College; **Hyunsook Jeong**, Keimyung University; **Mandy Kama**, Georgetown University; **Dale Kim**, Chung Dahm Institute; **Taeyoung Kim**, Keimyung University; **Woo-hyung Kim**, Keimyung University; **Young Kim**, Chung Dahm Institute; **Yu-kyung Kim**, Sunchon National University; **John Kostovich**, Miami Dade College; **Albert Kowun**, Fairfax, VA; **David Krise**, Michigan State University; **Cheri (Young Hee) Lee**, ReadingTownUSA English Language Institute; **Eun-Kyung Lee**, Chung Dahm Institute; **Sang Hyock Lee**, Keimyung University; **Debra Levitt**, SMC; **Karen Lewis**, Somerville, MA; **Chia-Hui Liu**, Wenzao Ursuline College of Languages; **Gennell Lockwood**, Seattle, WA; **Javier Lopez Anguiano**, Colegio Anglo Mexicano de Coyoacan; **Mary March**, Shoreline Community College; **Susan Matson**, ELS Language Centers; **Ralph McClain**, Embassy CES Boston; **Veronica McCormack**, Roxbury Community College; **Jennifer McCoy**, Kaplan; **Joseph McHugh**, Kaplan; **Cynthia McKeag Tsukamoto**, Oakton Community College; **Paola Medina**, Texas Southern University; **Christine Kyung-ah Moon**, Seoul, Korea; **Margaret Moore**, North Seattle Community College; **Michelle Moore**, Madison English as a Second Language School; **David Motta**, Miami University; **Suzanne Munro**, Clackamas Community College; **Elena Nehrbecki**, Hudson County CC; **Kim Newcomer**, University of Washington; **Melody Nightingale**, Santa Monica College; **Patrick Northover**, Kaplan Test and Prep; **Sarah Oettle**, Kaplan, Sacramento; **Shirley Ono**, Oakton Community College; **Maria Estela Ortiz Torres**, C. Anglo Mexicano de Coyoac'an; **Suzanne Overstreet**, West Valley College; **Linda Ozarow**, West Orange High School; **Ileana Porges-West**, Miami Dade College, Hialeah Campus; **Megan Power**, ILCSA; **Alison Robertson**, Cypress College; **Ma. Del Carmen Romero**, Universidad del Valle de Mexico; **Nina Rosen**, Santa Rosa Junior College; **Daniellah Salario**, Kaplan; **Joel Samuels**, Kaplan New York City; **Babi Sarapata**, Columbia University ALP; **Donna Schaeffer**, University of Washington; **Lynn Schneider**, City College of San Francisco; **Errol Selkirk**, New School University; **Amity Shook**, Chung Dahm Institute; **Lynn Stafford-Yilmaz**, Bellevue Community College; **Lynne Ruelaine Stokes**, Michigan State University; **Henna Suh**, Chung Dahm Institute; **Sheri Summers**, Kaplan Test Prep; **Martha Sutter**, Kent State University; **Becky Tarver Chase**, MESLS; **Lisa Waite-Trago**, Michigan State University; **Carol Troy**, Da-Yeh University; **Luci Tyrell**, Embassy CES Fort Lauderdale; **Yong-Hee Uhm**, Myongii University; **Debra Un**, New York University; **José Vazquez**, The University of Texas Pan American; **Hollyahna Vettori**, Santa Rosa Junior College; **Susan Vik**, Boston University; **Sandy Wagner**, Fort Lauderdale High School; **Joanne Wan**, ASC English; **Pat Wiggins**, Clackamas Community College; **Heather Williams**, University of Pennsylvania; **Carol Wilson-Duffy**, Michigan State University; **Kailin Yang**, Kaohsing Medical University; **Ellen Yaniv**, Boston University; **Samantha Young**, Kaplan Boston; **Yu-san Yu**, National Sun Yat-sen University; **Ann Zaaijer**, West Orange High School

The Friendship Page

Canada

New Zealand

FOCUS ON THE TOPIC

A PREDICT

Look at the picture. Discuss the questions with the class.

1. Where are the people?

2. What are they doing?

3. The title of this unit is "The Friendship Page." What is The Friendship Page?

1 *Look at the chart.*

How do people in the U.S. use the Internet?

Seventy percent (70%) of adults in the U.S. use the Internet. That's 141 million people. Here are some things they do online.

INTERNET USE[1] People use the Internet to . . .		PERCENTAGE OF INTERNET USERS
Buy something	✓	71%
Download music	✓	27%
Get news	✓	67%
Make travel plans	✓	63%
Play games online		35%
Sell something		15%
Send instant messages (IMs)	✓	39%
Send or read e-mail	✓	91%
Use a search engine, like Google®	✓	91%
Use a website like MySpace®, Facebook®, or Friendster®	✓	16%

[1] *Source:* www.pewInternet.org/trends/Internet_Activities_1.11.07.htm as of January 2007

2 *Answer the questions and complete the sentences. Compare your answers with a partner's.*

1. Look at the chart. How do most people use the Internet?

   1 ___email___ and ___else a search engine___

   2 ___Buy something___

   3 ___Get news___

2. Do you use the Internet? ___a___

   a. Yes, I use the Internet to ___do many things___

   b. No, I don't like the Internet.

   c. No, I don't have a computer.

   d. Your answer: _____.

C BACKGROUND AND VOCABULARY

Read the sentences. Then circle the definition of the boldfaced word.

1. Bronwyn wants to help her **community** in Melbourne. She wants to help people in other countries, too.

   A community is ____.
   a. all the people in one place
   b. all the people that you know

2. The movie last night was great! I **laughed** all night. I was so happy.

   You laugh when something is ____.
   a. sad
   b. funny

3. On The Friendship Page, people can write about their **goals**: a good job, a lot of money, a big family.

   A goal is ____.
   a. a problem you have now
   b. something you want in the future

(continued on next page)

4. When no one is fighting, people can live in **peace**.

   When you have peace, there is _____.
   a. quiet, agreement
   b. anger, disagreement

5. Karen likes The Friendship Page. She wants to **meet** new friends.

   When you meet people, you _____.
   a. call them on the telephone
   b. see or know them for the first time

6. Everyone has problems sometimes. Some people get **advice** on The Friendship Page.

   When you get advice, you get _____.
   a. helpful ideas
   b. money from your job

7. "Have no friends not equal to yourself" is a **quote** from Confucius (551–497 BC), a Chinese philosopher.

   A quote is _____.
   a. someone's problems
   b. someone's words

8. The Friendship Page is **safe** for young people and adults. Bronwyn and her helpers watch The Friendship Page very carefully.

   When something is safe, it is _____.
   a. not dangerous to use
   b. very easy to use

9. Bronwyn and her helpers are **volunteers**. No one gets money for working on The Friendship Page.

   Volunteers are _____.
   a. people who get money for working
   b. people who don't get money for working

10. People on The Friendship Page like to **chat** about family, work, and friends.

    When friends chat, they _____ together.
    a. talk or write
    b. visit or travel

H.W   • Find a website
       • write 3 products ——> name
       • payment methods —> price
              VISA - paypal - Debit etc

② FOCUS ON READING

Bronwyn Polson is from Melbourne, Australia. She started The Friendship Page, a website about friendship. Read this description of The Friendship Page:

"Everything you want to know about friends and friendships."
—The Australian Net Guide

Look at this part of Bronwyn's website.

1 Before you read, think about The Friendship Page. What is on this website? Check (✓) your ideas. Then read "Welcome to The Friendship Page" by Bronwyn Polson.

___✓___ advice   _____ pictures

___✓___ chat   ___✓___ poems

_____ e-mail addresses   ___✓___ songs

_____ information about Australia   _____ telephone numbers

___✓___ jokes   _____ other: _____

_____ people's real names

The Friendship Page

friendship.com.au

Welcome to The Friendship Page

1. Welcome to The Friendship Page—the website about friendship.

2. When I was 16 years old, I wanted to help my **community**. People **laughed**! They said, "You can't help. You are too young!" But I didn't listen to them.

3. I was sure that friendship is important to everyone. So, in 1996, I started The Friendship Page.

4. The Friendship Page has two **goals**. One goal is to make the Internet friendlier[1]. The other goal is to bring more **peace** to the world. The Friendship Page is really about "peace through friendship."

5. Today, 20 **volunteers** help me with The Friendship Page. We all work hard, but we have a lot of fun. We think our work is very important.

6. The Friendship Page is very popular. More than 13,000 people in 190 countries visit every day. That's 4,700,000 people every year.

7. The Friendship Page is friendly, free, fun, and easy to use. You can make new friends. You can get **advice** about friendship. There are interesting pages with songs, poems, **quotes**, jokes, and more. You can also **meet** new and old friends in the **chat** room.

8. People from 8 to 88 years old visit The Friendship Page. Most people are 13–34 years old. Young people and old people can be friends. They can help each other and learn a lot. Fifty-five percent are female, and 45 percent are male.

9. The Friendship Page is very **safe**. The volunteers watch the website carefully. They want it to be safe for everyone, especially for young people. We talk to the Australian police about Internet safety, too. On The Friendship Page, we do not use our real names. There are also no **personal** e-mail addresses, no phone numbers, and no personal pictures. Also, when you delete information from The Friendship Page, no one can see it again. The information does not stay on the Internet. This is not true of other websites like MySpace and Facebook.

10. If you are interested in friendship, please visit the The Friendship Page at www.friendship.com.au.

---

[1] **friendlier:** more friendly

2 *Now look at your answers to Question 1 on page 5. Were your answers correct?*

◖ READ FOR MAIN IDEAS

*Circle the **two correct answers** to complete each sentence.*

1. According to the reading, the two goals of The Friendship Page are _____ and _____.
   a. to make the Internet friendlier
   b. to work very hard
   c. to bring more peace to the world
   d. to make a lot of money

2. The Friendship Page is _____ and _____.
   a. safe
   b. friendly
   c. difficult to use
   d. old

◖ READ FOR DETAILS

Complete the sentences with the correct numbers from the reading.

1. The Friendship Page started in __1996__.

2. __70__ volunteers help Bronwyn with The Friendship Page.

3. __13,000__ people visit The Friendship Page every day.

4. __4,700,000__ people visit The Friendship Page every year.

5. People from __190__ countries use The Friendship Page.

6. People from __8__ to __88__ years old use The Friendship Page.

7. __55__ percent are girls or women. __45__ percent are boys or men.

◖ MAKE INFERENCES

*Work with a partner. Read each sentence. Write **T** (true) or **F** (false). Then share your answers with the class.*

__F__ 1. People agree that 16-year-old kids can help the community.

__T__ 2. Bronwyn has a lot of friends.

__T__ 3. Today, many people think The Friendship Page is a good idea.

__T__ 4. Some websites are not safe.

Do you want to visit The Friendship Page? Check (✓) your answer. Then choose a reason or add your ideas. Share your answer with a partner.

_____ Yes, I want to visit The Friendship Page.

- I like to meet friends online.
- The Friendship Page is safe.
- ✓ I like the goals of The Friendship Page.
- _____

_____ No, I don't want to visit The Friendship Page.

- I don't like to meet friends online.
- It is not safe to meet people online.
- I don't want more friends.
- _____

Meeting a friend online

Meeting a friend in person

Read the passage about MySpace.

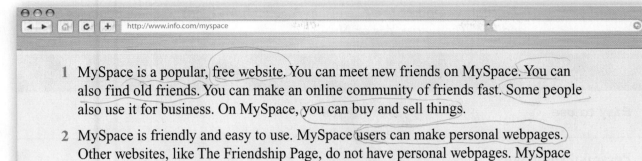

1 MySpace is a popular, free website. You can meet new friends on MySpace. You can also find old friends. You can make an online community of friends fast. Some people also use it for business. On MySpace, you can buy and sell things.

2 MySpace is friendly and easy to use. MySpace users can make personal webpages. Other websites, like The Friendship Page, do not have personal webpages. MySpace users can visit your personal webpage and chat with you.

3 MySpace started in 2003. Today, more than 100 million people from more than 14 countries use MySpace. Most users are 16–54 years old. They must be 14 years or older, but it is difficult to check. Forty-nine percent of MySpace users are female and 51 percent are male. There are more than 50,000 interesting groups, like health, sports, music, and TV.

4 Some people say that there are two problems. First, there is no one to watch MySpace carefully to make it safe for everyone. Second, other Internet companies can copy your personal information and pictures. Your personal information can stay on the Internet long after you stop using MySpace. But MySpace is still very popular. Visit MySpace (www.MySpace.com) for more information.

*Write **T** (true) or **F** (false).*

_F_ **1.** People pay $10 to use MySpace.

_T_ **2.** You can meet friends on MySpace.

_T_ **3.** You can sell things on MySpace.

_T_ **4.** Users have personal webpages on MySpace.

_F_ **5.** Volunteers watch MySpace to make it safe.

◀ STEP 1: Organize

*The chart compares The Friendship Page with MySpace. Review Readings One and Two. Then write **Yes** or **No**.*

	THE FRIENDSHIP PAGE	MYSPACE
Easy to use	Yes	yes
Personal webpages	No	yes
Fun	Yes	yes
Friendly	Yes	yes
Males and females	Yes	yes
Users of different ages	Yes	yes
OK to use for business	No	yes
Safe for young users	Yes	No
Interesting pages or groups	Yes	yes
Free for users	Yes	yes
Problems	No	yes

Imagine that you are Bronwyn Polson. Use the information in the chart to complete the answers.

1. Do you like The Friendship Page?

   Of course I do!

   The Friendship Page is _____ Frendly _____.

   It has _____ more then 13,000 users _____.

   Users can _____ meet friends _____.

2. Do you like MySpace?

   Yes, I do!

   MySpace is _____ Free _____.

   It has _____ more then 100 million _____.

   Users can _____ buy and sell things _____.

3. Is there a problem with The Friendship Page?

   Well, maybe a small one.

   The Friendship Page needs _____ Volunteers _____

   and _____ hard work _____.

   We need help!

4. Is there a problem with MySpace?

   MySpace is not always _____ Private _____.

   People need to be careful with their personal information.

is — cadj

has — noun

can — verb

H.w ① choose a social media
② write about its Pros and cons
↳ 4sentences

③ FOCUS ON WRITING

Ⓐ VOCABULARY

◖ REVIEW

Read the paragraph. Then fill in the blanks with words from the box.

advice	laughed	quotes
chat	meet	safe
community	peace	users
~~goal~~	personal	volunteers

At 16, Bronwyn Polson's _____goal_____ was to do something good for her

1.

___Community___ and for the world. Bronwyn called newspapers and social service

2.

organizations, but they just ___laughed___. They said she was too young to help.

3.

So, she started a website called The Friendship Page. She believes in

"___peace___ through friendship." On The Friendship Page people

4.

___meet___ new friends. They can ___chat___ about important things.

5.   6.

It has ___advice___ for people with friendship problems. The ___quotes___

7.   8.

page is the most popular part.

___Volunteers___ help Bronwyn. They want The Friendship Page to be

9.

___safe___ for everyone. ___users___ do not give important

10.   11.

___personal___ information. The Friendship Page is a lot of work, but Bronwyn

12.

enjoys it very much.

When you meet people, you **greet** them (you say hello), and then you say a little more. It is important to greet someone correctly. It is also important to say good-bye correctly. Use these expressions "in person" (face to face), online, or on the phone.

SITUATIONS	EXPRESSIONS
Meeting someone for the first time (in person or online)	It's nice to meet you. Nice to meet you.
Meeting someone for the second time (in person or online)	Nice to meet you again.
Meeting someone for the second time or more (in person)	Nice to see you again.
Saying good-bye to a new friend	It was nice to meet you. (in person or online) Nice meeting you. (in person or online) Nice talking to you. (in person or on the phone) Nice chatting with you. (in a chat or on the phone)

Complete the conversations with the expressions from Expand. Sometimes more than one answer is possible.

1. **(in an online chat room or face to face)**

   JEFF: Hi, my name is Jeff.

   YOU: _____. My name is

   _____.

   JEFF: _____, too.

2. **(at a party)**

   JANET: Hi, I'm Janet. We met last year at Jeff's birthday party.

   YOU: Oh, that's right. _____, Janet.

(continued on next page)

3. **(in an online chat room or face to face)**

   JACK: Well, I have to run.

   YOU: OK. _____.

   JACK: You, too. Thanks. _____, too.

4. **(on the phone)**

   YOU: Hello?

   JACKIE: Hi. This is Jackie, Janet's friend.

   YOU: Hi, Jackie. I'm glad you called.

   (You and Jackie talk for 10 minutes.)

   JACKIE: OK, I'll let you go.

   YOU: OK. _____. Thanks for calling.

   JACKIE: Bye now.

   YOU: Bye.

◖ CREATE

A **screen name** is the special name you use online, like "GoodStudent" or "TerryTerrific." Think of a screen name for yourself. Use your screen name in this activity.

You are in a Friendship Page chat room with GoodStudent. You met GoodStudent last week for the first time. Today GoodStudent introduces you to TerryTerrific. Talk about The Friendship Page together. Complete the conversation. Use the vocabulary from Review and Expand. Practice your conversation with two partners.

✦ ✦ The Friendship Page   ✦ ✦ ✦ ✦ friendship.com.au

Friendship Chat

GS: Hi, _____.
      (your screen name)

YOU: Hi, GoodStudent. _____.
      (Say hello with "Nice …")

GS: You too! _____, this is my
      (your screen name)

      friend TerryTerrific.

      TerryTerrific, this is _____.
      (your screen name)

TT: Nice _____.
      (Say hello with "Nice …")

You: Nice _____, too. I like your
(Say hello with "Nice …")
screen name. It's terrific!

I know GoodStudent is in Sydney. Where are you from, Terry?

TT: I am in Seoul, South Korea. Where

_____?
(Ask the same question.)

You: I'm in _____.
(your city or country)

TT: Isn't this great? I like The Friendship Page. It

_____.
(Give a positive opinion about The Friendship Page.)

You: Yes, and I can _____.
(Write something you can do on The Friendship Page.)

GS: Yes, and _____.
(Write another thing you can do on The Friendship Page.)
Wow! It's 11:00 A.M. here. I have class.

You: And I have to sleep!

TT: OK. I have to go, too. _____
(Say good-bye with "Nice …")
both.

You: _____, TerryTerrific.
(Say good-bye with "Nice …")

Nice _____, GoodStudent.
(Say good-bye with "Nice …")

TT: Bye.

GS: Later! ☺

You: See ya.

2 *Practice your conversation with two partners.*

B **GRAMMAR: Questions with *Be* and *Have***

1 *Read the questions (Q) and answers (A).*

   1. Q: <u>Is</u> The Friendship Page a website?

      A: Yes, it <u>is</u>. It <u>is</u> a website about friendship.

   2. Q: Who is Bronwyn Polson?

      A: She is a young woman from Australia.   *(continued on next page)*

3. **Q:** Am I too young to help?

   A: No, you aren't.

4. **Q:** Does Bronwyn have a lot of friends?

   A: Yes, she does. She has a lot of friends on The Friendship Page.

5. **Q:** Do users have trouble using The Friendship Page?

   A: No, they don't. They don't have trouble using it.

2 *Look at the questions and answers in 1 again. Underline the verbs, including the helping verbs, twice. Underline the subjects once.*

QUESTIONS WITH *BE*	
1. For **yes / no questions**, use: the verb ***be* + subject** You can answer *yes / no* questions with a short answer. Don't use contractions in short answers with *yes*.	[verb] [subject] **Is** The Friendship Page a website? [subject] [verb] Yes, it **is**. [verb] [subject] **Am** I too young to help? [subject][verb] Yes, you **are**. NOT: ~~Yes, you're.~~ [subject][verb] No, you**'re** not. [subject][verb] No, you **aren't**.
2. For **wh- questions**, use: ***Wh-* word + *be* + subject**	[verb] [subject] Who **is** Bronwyn Polson? [verb] [subject] What **is** The Friendship Page? [verb] [subject] When **is** your birthday? [verb][subject] Where **are** they from? [verb] [subject] How old **is** The Friendship Page?

QUESTIONS WITH *HAVE*

1. For *yes / no* questions, use:

do / does + subject + have

$$\begin{bmatrix} \text{helping} \\ \text{verb} \end{bmatrix} \quad \text{[subject]} \quad \begin{bmatrix} \text{main} \\ \text{verb} \end{bmatrix}$$

	I	
Do	you	**have** a lot of friends?
	we	
	they	
Does	she	**have** a goal?
	he	

You can answer *yes / no* questions with a short answer.

Does she **have** a goal?
   Yes, she does.
   No, she doesn't.
Do you **have** a lot of friends?
   Yes, I do.
   No, I don't.

2. For *wh-* questions, use:

Wh- word + do / does + subject

$$\begin{bmatrix} \text{helping} \\ \text{verb} \end{bmatrix} \quad \text{[subject]} \quad \begin{bmatrix} \text{main} \\ \text{verb} \end{bmatrix}$$

What does The Friendship Page **have** on it?
   It **has** jokes, quotes, and much more.

$$\begin{bmatrix} \text{helping} \\ \text{verb} \end{bmatrix} \quad \begin{bmatrix} \text{main} \\ \text{verb} \end{bmatrix}$$
$$\text{[subject]}$$

Remember to end questions with a question mark (**?**).

How many friends does she **have**?
   She **has** many friends.

---

3 Write questions about The Friendship Page. Then give your questions to a partner. Ask your partner to write the answers.

1. The Friendship Page / be / a website?

   Is The Friendship Page a website?

2. Friendship Page users / have / personal webpages?

   Does Friendship Page users have Personal...?

3. The Friendship Page / have / a chat room?

   Does the Friendship Page have a chat room?

4. Bronwyn Polson / have / a goal?

   Does Bronwyn Polson have a goal?

5. What / be / Bronwyn's goal?

   What is Bronwyn's goal?

(continued on next page)

6. How old / be / The Friendship
   Page?

   How old is the friendship page?

7. Who / be / Bronwyn Polson?

   Who is Bronwyn Polson?

8. Bronwyn / be / from England?

   Is Bronwyn from England?

9. Where / be / Bronwyn / from?

   Where is Bronwyn from?

10. Bronwyn Polson / have / people
    to help her?

    Does Bronwyn Polson have people to help her

11. How old / be / you?

    How old are you?

12. Where / be / you / from?

    Where are you form?

13. You / have / one best friend?

    Do you have one best friend?

14. Who / be / your best friend(s)?

    Who is your best frind?
    who are your best friends?

15. You / have / a personal
    webpage on MySpace?

    Do you have a personal webpage on my space?

Your partner's answers:

1. Yes, it is.
2. *No, they don't*
3. *Yes, it does*
4. *Yes, she does*
5. *Bronwyn's goal is to do some-thing good for her community and world*
6. *The friendship page is 18 years old. OR it is 18 years old*
7. *She is creat or of Friendship page.*
8. *No, she is not*
9. *She is form Australia I think.*
10. *yes, she does*
11. *I'm ---- years old.*
12. *I'm from Libya.*
13. *Yes, I do*
14. *He is.. my frind*
15. *No, I don't*

In this unit, you read about two websites where people meet and make friends.

You are going to **write a paragraph about a classmate and one of his or her friends**. Use the vocabulary and grammar from the unit.*

PREPARE TO WRITE: Interviewing

To learn about another person, you are going to do a prewriting activity called **interviewing**. In an interview, you ask questions. Then you use the information from the interview when you write.

Interview a classmate. Ask questions using the words provided and the correct form of **be** *and* **have**. *Write the answers in complete sentences on a separate piece of paper.*

1. What / be / your name?   *what is your name   yasef*
2. Where / be / you from?   *suidi*   [are]
3. When / be / your birthday?   [is]   *1976*
4. You / have / a job? What / be / your job? Be / you / a student?   [Do]   [is]   [Are]   *yes I do It is costomr servces yes I'm*
5. You / have / hobbies or interests? What / be / they?   [Do]   [are]   *yes I Do shoping and study English*
6. Who / be / your best friend?   [is]   *my best friend is mohamed*
7. Where / be / he (or she) from?   [is]
8. How old / be / he (or she)?   [is]
9. Your friend / have / a job? What / be / his (or her) job? Be / he (or she) / a student?   [Does]   [is]   [is]
10. What / be / his (or her) hobbies or interests?   [is]

His name is yosef he is from stydia Arabia his birthday is . . . . . and he is a student she has hobbies they are shoping and study English. and his best friend is himself .

---

*For Alternative Writing Topics, see page 24. These topics can be used in place of the writing topic for this unit or as homework. The alternative topics relate to the theme of the unit, but may not target the same grammar or rhetorical structures taught in the unit.

◀ **WRITE: A Sentence**

A **sentence** is a group of words that makes a statement or asks a question.

THE SENTENCE	
I. A sentence is a group of words that expresses a complete idea.	
2. A **sentence** has a **subject** and a **verb**.	[subject] [verb] **Bronwyn is** a university student. [subject] [verb] **Volunteers help** with The Friendship Page. [subject][verb] **I want** to write a book about friendship.
BUT: In **commands**, don't use a subject (*you*).	[verb] **Send** me an e-mail tomorrow.
3. The **first word** in a sentence begins with a **capital letter**.	**T**he website offers information and advice. **F**riendship is important to everyone.
4. Use a **period** at the end of a sentence. Use a **question mark** at the end of a question. Use an **exclamation point** at the end of a sentence with strong feeling.	The Friendship Page has fun information**.** Is this website safe**?** Wow**!** The Friendship Page is free**!**

for example I say
→Ali stand up

1 *Read the sentences. Underline the subjects once and the verbs twice. Add punctuation (a period, a question mark, or an exclamation point) at the end of each sentence.*

What Is Facebook_?_

Facebook is another popular website_._ Facebook started in 2004_._

It is really great_!_ Users have personal webpages_._ They chat with old

friends and meet new ones_._ Are you interested_?_ Visit Facebook

online for more information_._

Examples simple sentence

I Walk. ✓

2 *If the group of words is a sentence, check (✓)* **sentence**. *If not, check* **not a** **sentence**, *and change it to make it a sentence.*

	sentence	not a sentence
1. My friend's name is Jane [who] ^	___	✓
2. Urville and Vera are from Chicago.	✓	___
3. Tony [is] 23 years old.	___	✓
4. Is a good student. *is* [he/she] *a good student* — *subject*	___	✓
5. My sister likes playing basketball.	✓	___
6. I play basketball? ✓ *Do I Play basketball?*	✓	___
7. She has a lot of friends.	✓	___
8. My brother [is/The] my best friend.	___	✓
9. [We] we have fun on The Friendship Page.	___	✓
10. We like reading the jokes and the quotes.	✓	___

3 *Read the sentences. Find five more errors and correct them.*

(1) [M] ~~my~~ classmate's name is Bernard. (2) He is 24 years old. (3) He is from Senegal. (4) [He] Likes playing soccer and going dancing. (5) Bernard's best friend [is] Alexandre. (6) [H] he is from France. (7) He is intelligent and shy. (8) He likes going to the beach and reading. (9) Do you have any questions to ask him[?]

4 *Now write your* **first draft**. *Your first draft is the first time your write your ideas. Your first draft is different from your* **final draft**. *You will make some changes later. Begin like this:*

> "My classmate's name is . . . He is . . ."
>
> OR
>
> "My classmate's name is . . . His best friend is . . ."

◖ **REVISE:** Ordering Your Ideas

A group of sentences about one main idea is a **paragraph**.

Read the paragraphs. Then answer the questions.

> The Friendship Page is very safe. The volunteers watch the website carefully. They want it to be safe for everyone, especially for young people. We talk to the Australian police about Internet safety, too.

How many sentences are in this paragraph? __4__

> MySpace started in 2003. Today, more than 100 million people from more than 14 countries use MySpace. Most users are 16–54 years old. They must be 14 years or older, but it is difficult to check. Forty-nine percent of MySpace users are female and 51 percent are male. There are more than 50,000 interesting groups, like health, sports, music, and TV.

How many sentences are in this paragraph? __6__

When you write your paragraph, you can organize the information in different ways. Here are two: (1) person by person or (2) by ideas. Look at Description One and Description Two.

1 *Read Description One. It gives sentences about Fernando and then sentences about his friend, Ricardo. The order is "person by person."*

Description One

> My classmate's name is Fernando. He is from Spain. He is 21 years old. He is a student in Chicago. Fernando is friendly. He likes going to parties. Fernando's best friend is Ricardo. He is from Spain. He is 20 years old. He is a student in Madrid. Ricardo is friendly and athletic. He likes going to parties and playing sports.

2 Read Description Two. It gives information about Fernando and Ricardo together. The order is "by ideas."

Description Two

> My classmate's name is Fernando. His best friend is Ricardo. Fernando is from Spain. He is 21 years old. Ricardo is also from Spain. He is 20 years old. Fernando is a student in Chicago. Ricardo is a student in Madrid. Fernando and Ricardo are both friendly. They like going to parties. Ricardo also likes playing sports.

3 Read both Description One and Description Two again. For both descriptions,
- Underline the sentences about Fernando.
- Circle the sentences about Ricardo.
- Underline twice the sentences about both Fernando and Ricardo.

4 Look at your sentences from your interview. Order your ideas. Number the sentences. Organize your sentences like Description One or Description Two.

◖ **EDIT: Writing the Final Draft**

Prepare to write the final draft of your paragraph. Check your grammar, spelling, capitalization, and punctuation. Check that you used some of the vocabulary and grammar from the unit. Use the checklist to help you write your final draft. Then neatly write or type your paragraph.

✔ FINAL DRAFT CHECKLIST

- ○ Did you describe a classmate and his (or her) friend?
- ○ Did you use complete sentences?
- ○ Did you organize your information?
- ○ Did you use *be* and *have*?
- ○ Did you use vocabulary from the unit?

ALTERNATIVE WRITING TOPICS

Write about one of the topics. Use the vocabulary and grammar from the unit.

1. Bronwyn Polson has a goal. She wants "peace through friendship." She wants people to learn about friendship. Do you have a goal? It can be big or small, for the world or for yourself. Write three to five sentences about your goal. Begin with: *"In the future I want to (be a doctor/write a book) . . ."*

2. Do you have friends or family who live far away? How do you communicate with them: by e-mail or on the telephone? Write five sentences about communicating with these people.

3. Describe one of your good friends. Who is this person? Why are you friends? Look at the list. Check (✓) the most important qualities of your friend. Use your dictionary for help. Write five or more sentences about your friend.

Qualities of a Good Friend

____ funny

____ good-looking

____ helpful

____ honest

____ intelligent

____ patient

____ popular

____ talkative

____ your idea(s): _____

_____

_____

RESEARCH TOPICS, see page 218.

What Will I Wear?

1.

2.

3.

4.

5.

A

6.

7.

8.

9.

10.

B

dress pants ___5___

dress shirt ___3___

jacket ___ ___7___

jeans ___10___

polo shirt ___8___

blazer ___4___

school sweater ___1___

skirt ___2___

sweater ___9___

T-shirt ___6___

① FOCUS ON THE TOPIC

A PREDICT

Look at the picture. Discuss the questions with the class.

2 in Picture A

1. Which students are wearing a **school uniform**? Point to the students.

2. Label the pieces of clothing each person is wearing in pictures A and B. Write the numbers next to the words in the box.

3. Is a school uniform a good idea? Why or why not?

Look at the four students. Look at their clothes and the vocabulary in the box. Are their clothes OK for school? Write the number on the line. Then compare your answers with a partner's. Explain your choices using the words in the box.

| dress shoes | hat | sandals | sweatshirt | tie | vest |

Definitely	Probably	Probably not	Definitely not
OK for school	OK for school	OK for school	OK for school
1	2	3	4

 Emily

4 **Eric**

_2_ **Jason**

_3_ **Diane**

Public schools in the United States are free for all students. Most students in public schools do not wear uniforms. Private schools are not free. Students pay for private school. Most students in private schools wear uniforms. Some people think uniforms are a good idea, but other people do not.

1 _Look at the graph. Then answer the question below the graph._

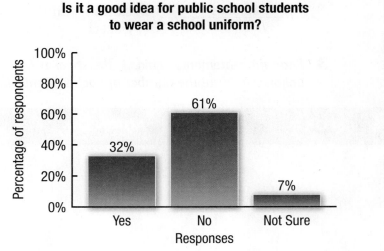

Is it a good idea for public school students to wear a school uniform?

Percentage of respondents

100%
80%
60% — 61%
40%
32%
20%
0%
7%

Yes   No   Not Sure
Responses

Source: Kids Zone: Learning with NCES, 2007

Do most people think a school uniform is a good idea or a bad idea?

2 Read the statements. *Match the boldfaced words with their definitions. Write the words on the lines.*

1. I want to wear my **clothes**. I don't like uniforms.

2. I like **designer** clothes—for example, Calvin Klein or Armani or Prada.

3. Students in uniforms work together and have group **spirit**.

4. **Fashion** is important to me. I like to wear different clothes.

5. Baseball and soccer **teams** wear uniforms. School is not a sport!

6. Designer clothes are **expensive**.

7. Students in a uniform look very **neat** and clean.

8. Well, maybe a school uniform will **increase** group spirit.

9. Students will not be **comfortable** in jackets and ties all day!

Comfortable **a.** easy to wear

Fashion **b.** clothing, eyeglasses, etc. popular at a certain time

teams **c.** groups that play or work together

spirit **d.** a happy feeling of being together with other people

increase **e.** become more

designer **f.** made by a famous person or clothing company

expensive **g.** having a high price

neat **h.** in order, not messy

clothes **i.** clothing, things you wear such as shirts, pants, and jackets

3 Read the statements again. *Is the speaker for or against or not sure about school uniforms? Write the number of each sentence in the correct column.*

FOR	AGAINST	NOT SURE
3	1,	5
6	2	
7	4	
8		
9		

② FOCUS ON READING

A READING ONE: A Letter from the Principal

*Read only the first sentence of Mr. Collins' letter. Then check (✓) the **true** sentence.*

_____ Mr. Collins is asking students and parents about a school uniform.

✓ Mr. Collins is telling students and parents about a uniform.

LINCOLN HIGH SCHOOL

Mr. Peter F. Collins
Principal
Lincoln High School
2064 School Street
Salem, New Hampshire 03079

Dear Students and Parents:

Next year, all students at Lincoln High School will wear a school uniform.

Boys and girls will wear a white shirt and a dark blue jacket. Boys will also wear a blue tie and dark gray pants. Girls will wear dark gray pants or a dark gray skirt.

Wearing a uniform is a good idea. The uniform will help students study hard. They will think about school and school work, not about **fashion**. Today, students think too much about **clothes** and how they look. It is important to think about education first.

Uniforms also look **neat** and clean. When students are neat and clean, they are more **comfortable**. When they are more comfortable, they study more.

Uniforms will also **increase** school **spirit**. Students in uniforms will look like a team, and they will work together as a team.

Uniforms are also less **expensive** than popular **designer** clothes. Parents will be happy about that. Parents can buy the new school uniform at Benson's Department Store on Broadway in the Salem Shopping Center.

Enjoy your summer vacation.

Sincerely,

Peter F. Collins

Peter F. Collins

◀ READ FOR MAIN IDEAS

Read the entire letter on page 29. Circle the correct answer to complete the sentence.

Mr. Collins _____.

a. wants to wear a school uniform
b. does not want students to wear a uniform
c. wants students to wear a uniform

◀ READ FOR DETAILS

Complete the sentences. Use each word only once.

blue	expensive	gray	spirit
comfortable	fashion	neat	white

In his letter, Mr. Collins writes:

1. The colors of the uniform are ___blue___, ___gray___, and ___white___.
2. Students think about ___fashion___ too much.
3. Uniforms are not ___expensive___.
4. Uniforms are ___comfortable___ and ___neat___ to wear.
5. School uniforms increase school ___spirit___.

◀ MAKE INFERENCES

*Write **T** (true) or **F** (false). Talk about your answers.*

__F__ 1. Students at Lincoln High have a uniform this year.

__T__ 2. Parents want to spend less money on clothes.

__T__ 3. Mr. Collins thinks school spirit is important.

__F__ 4. Students at Lincoln High chose the colors of the new uniform.

__F__ 5. Mr. Collins wants to know the opinions of students and parents.

◀ EXPRESS OPINIONS

In his letter, Mr. Collins gives reasons why he wants to have a school uniform. In your opinion, which reasons in his letter are good? Which are bad? Write his reasons in the chart on the next page. Compare your answers with a partner's.

GOOD REASONS	BAD REASONS
neat *increase spirit* *comfortable* *Less expensive*	

B READING TWO: School Newspaper Editorial

1 *Read the editorial by a student at Lincoln High School.*

THE LINCOLN TIMES

The Newspaper of Lincoln High School
By Samantha Lin, Editor

This week Principal Peter Collins wrote a letter to students and parents at Lincoln High. In his letter, Mr. Collins says that students will wear a uniform starting next year. This is a bad idea.

Mr. Collins says uniforms are less expensive than designer clothes. Maybe this is true, but not all students have designer clothes. And some uniforms are more expensive than other clothes.

More important, uniforms decrease school spirit. There will be no individuality—students in uniforms all look the same and feel the same. This is really bad. Students want to feel special. Fashion gives students individuality. Sometimes we don't want to be neat—sometimes we want to be messy. For some students, messy is comfortable.

Next year students at Lincoln High will all look and feel the same: bad. Principal Collins needs to change his plan. Please call his office and tell him your opinion.

2 *Work with a partner. Answer the questions.*

1. Does Samantha Lin agree or disagree with Mr. Collins?

2. How do you know? *This is bad idea and some uniforms are mor expensive*

C INTEGRATE READINGS ONE AND TWO

STEP 1: Organize

*Look at Readings One and Two again. Write the ideas **for** and **against** school uniforms in the chart.*

FOR UNIFORMS	AGAINST UNIFORMS
will help students study hard *Uniform Less expensive*	*some uniform clothes are expensive*

STEP 2: Synthesize

Role-play. Work with a partner. One partner is Mr. Collins, and the other is the parent of a student at Lincoln High School. Imagine that you go to Principal Collins' office to talk about the new uniform. Continue the conversation.

PARENT: [*knock, knock . . .*] Mr. Collins?

COLLINS: Yes, Mr./Mrs./Ms. _____! Come in. Please, sit down.

(last name)

PARENT: Thank you.

COLLINS: What can I do for you today?

PARENT: I want to talk about the school uniform.

COLLINS: Yes, the uniform. [*smiling*] The kids don't like the idea too much.

PARENT: Well, I agree with the kids.

COLLINS: Oh, really?

PARENT: Yes. I don't think having a uniform is a good idea because

_____ Some uniform are expenseve. _____

COLLINS: But ___will help students study hard._____

PARENT: _____

COLLINS: _____

PARENT: _____

COLLINS: _____

PARENT: _____

COLLINS: _____

3 FOCUS ON WRITING

A VOCABULARY

REVIEW

Complete the sentences by unscrambling the boldfaced words.

1. I love to wear my blue shirt. It's very **baceflmoort**. _confortable_

2. *Vogue* is a famous **hafinos** magazine. _fasions_

3. Giorgio Armani is a famous **gedenirs**. _designer_

4. The number of students **saceeinrs** every year, but the number of teachers **sacedeers**. _increases_ , _decreases_

5. Barbara's clothes are always **enta**, but Bob's clothes are very **seysm**. _neate_ , _messy_

6. I have a lot of **chelost** in my closet. _clothes_

7. I am on the baseball **meat** at my school. _team_

8. School **pistir** is important. _spirit_

9. Our fashion shows our **yaiddlinituvi**. _individuality_

10. Gucci shoes are too **inpesvexe** for me to buy. _expensive_

You **put on** specific pieces of clothing.

When you **get dressed,** you put on all your clothes for the day.

Debbie **puts on** her school uniform in the morning.

If I am cold, I **put on** a sweater.

She **gets dressed** at 7:00 each day.

I **get dressed** before I eat breakfast.

You **wear** clothes or pieces of clothing (*after* you put them on).

Debbie **wears** a uniform at school every day.

He **is wearing** a suit right now.

Complete the sentences. Share your answers with a partner.

1. Every morning before breakfast, I _____get dressed_____.

2. When I feel cold in class, I _____put on a sweater._____.

3. When you play on the baseball team, you _____wear sport clothe_____

*Write five sentences about the person in the pictures. Use **put on, get dressed,** or **wear** and some of the words from the box.*

clothes	designer	increase	neat	uniform
comfortable	equal	individuality	spirit	wear
decrease	fashion	messy	team	

1. In the morning he ___Puts on~~his~~ uniform.___
2. At work ___he wears uniform.~~clothes~~___
3. After work ___he wears traditional clothes___
4. He (not) ___He ~~doesn't~~ isn't wearing uniform after work___
5. ___always wears his fire fighter, becuse it makes___
   ___him feel like he's on a team___

What Will I Wear?   **35**

1 Look at Reading Two on page 31. How many sentences use **will**? Write the sentences on the lines.

Students will wear a uniform starting next year.

There will be no individuality-students in uniforms all look
the same and feel the same.

will all look and feel the same.

THE FUTURE WITH *WILL*	
1. Use **will** before the base verb to talk about the future.	Next year, students at Lincoln High **will wear** a school uniform. (v) They **will think** about school work, not about clothes. (v) Uniforms **will** also **increase** school spirit. (v) Students **will work** together as a team. (v)
2. For negative sentences, use **will not** or **won't** before the base verb.	We **will not wear** a uniform at work! It's too uncomfortable. (a) (aj) Karen **won't buy** designer clothes. They are too expensive. (aj) (aj)
3. For questions, put **will** before the subject.	**Will you go** to Benson's Department Store with me? What **will you wear** to work at Hamburger Hut?

2 Write your answers in complete sentences.

1. Will you be home tonight at 9:00 P.M.? _____ I will be home tonight at 9:00_

2. When (at what time) will you go home today? _I will go home today_

3. Will you do your homework tonight? _Yes, I will do my homework tonight_

4. When will you go shopping for clothes? _I will go shopping for clothes next week_

5. When you need help, who will help you? _I need help in this class. My teacher will help me._

6. Who will you call on the telephone next? _I will call my brother on the telephone_

7. Will you take a vacation soon? _I will take a vacation soon?_

8. When (in what year) will you be 100 years old? _I will be 100 years old in 2080_

9. Where will you be tomorrow at 9:00 A.M.? _I will be U of C tomorrow at 9:00 AM_

10. What time will you have dinner tonight? _I will have dinner tonight at 10:00 pm_

C WRITING

> In this unit, you read a letter from the school principal telling students about the new school uniform.
>
> You are going to **write a letter to the head of your school, your child's school, or your workplace.** Describe a uniform or dress code[1] that you think is a good idea. What will students (or employees) wear? Why will this uniform or dress code be OK? Use the vocabulary and grammar from the unit.*

PREPARE TO WRITE: Brainstorming

To help you think of a topic for your paragraph, you are going to do a prewriting activity called **brainstorming**. When brainstorming, you quickly make a list of ideas. You don't stop to think about your ideas. You just add to your list. After brainstorming, look at the list and choose the ideas that you want to keep.

1. Look at your topic. What place will you write about: your school, your child's school, your workplace, or someplace else?

2. On a piece of paper, brainstorm a list of clothes people wear now at this place.

3. On a piece of paper, brainstorm a list of clothes people will wear (your plan).

---

[1] **a dress code:** a set of rules about clothes students or employees can and cannot wear (not as specific as a uniform)

*For Alternative Writing Topics, see page 42. These topics can be used in place of the writing topic for this unit or as homework. The alternative topics relate to the theme of the unit, but may not target the same grammar or rhetorical structures taught in the unit.

◖ WRITE: A Letter with an Opinion

To give an opinion, use *I think (that)* _____.

In formal writing, use **that**.

In everyday speaking, you do not have to use **that**.

1 *Work with a partner. Take turns asking and answering the questions. Give your opinion. Is it a good idea or a bad idea? Do not write your answers.*

ASK: Do you think _____ is a good idea or a bad idea?

ANSWER: I think _____ is a (good / bad) idea.

1. free food at school

2. more vacation days

3. more homework

4. longer classes

5. a school uniform

6. a dress code at school

7. a uniform for police officers and firefighters

8. a uniform for flight attendants

2 *Write your answers to the questions in Exercise 1. Use **I think that . . .***

1. I think that is a good idea.

2. I think that is a bad idea

3. I think that is a good idea

4. I think that isn't a good idea

5. I think that is a good and important

6. I think that isn't good

7. I think that a uniform for plice officers and firefighters

8. I think that a uniform ——— is a good idea

Disn't always a good idea

When you give an opinion, you often give a reason. When you give a reason, use **because**.

Uniforms are a bad idea **because** students will be unhappy.

3 *Complete the sentences.*

1. Free books for students is a (*good / bad*) idea because

   I think that free books for students is a good idea, becuse they can save money.

2. Fifty-minute classes are a (*good / bad*) idea because

   I think that fifty minute classes are a bad idea becuse students need time for rest.

3. Buying designer clothes is a (*good / bad*) idea because

   I think that ↑ bad idea, becuse they aren't comfortable.

4. Wearing jeans at school is a (*good / bad*) idea because

   I thing that ↑ bad idea, because

5. A police officer in a uniform is a (*good / bad*) idea because

   I thing that ↑ bad idea, becuse the thife will know thim

6. A waitress in a uniform is a (*good / bad*) idea because

   _____

   _____

7. _____

   is a (*good / bad*) idea because _____

   _____

4 *Get ready to write your letter. Answer the questions in complete sentences. Remember to choose one situation: at your school, at your child's school, or at your workplace.*

1. What do people wear now?

   _____

2. Is this a good idea or a bad idea? Why?

   _____

3. What is the best idea (uniform / dress code / no dress code)?

   _____

4. Why will this plan be better?

   _____

5 *Write the first draft of your letter. Complete the letter with the sentences you wrote in Exercise 4.*

Dear _____ director _____:
        (name)

I am writing to give my opinion about clothing at

university of calgary .
        (school / work)

Today people at _____ U of C _____ wear
                        (the place)

mini skirts and costumes to _____ U of C _____. I think
                                        (school / work)

that . . . this clothing is innppropriate .

because students can't focus on their studies

In my plan, _____ students _____ will wear . . . a school
        (students / workers / people / etc.)

uniform include dress

_____

_____ .

Sincerely,

_____
        (your name)

REVISE: The Order of Descriptive Adjectives

Use **descriptive adjectives** to "make a picture" with words. The chart shows the order of descriptive adjectives.

	Opinion	Physical Description	Color	Pattern	Material	
She has on (a) **He is wearing (a)**	comfortable neat messy *Cheap* *beautiful* *strange* *an ugly* *nice*	bright dark heavy light light-weight short short-sleeved long-sleeved	black blue green	checked plaid striped polka-dot *floral* *solid*	cotton polyester silk wool *leather*	**shirt** **pants**

Examples

[opinion] [physical description] [color][pattern] [material]

He has on a comfortable bright blue striped cotton shirt.

[color][material]

She is wearing black wool pants.

Complete the tasks.

1. Describe the clothes you have on today. Start with *Today I am wearing* or *Today I have on . . .*

   _____

2. Describe what someone in your class has on today. Write your description on the lines. Then describe the person to the class. Let the class decide who the person is.

   _____

   _____

3. Look back at your first draft. Make sure you use descriptive adjectives in your letter.

◖EDIT: Writing the Final Draft

Prepare to write the final draft of your letter. Check your grammar, spelling, capitalization, and punctuation. Check that you used some of the vocabulary and grammar from the unit. Use the checklist to help you write your final draft. Then neatly write or type your letter.

✓ FINAL DRAFT CHECKLIST

❍ Did you write a letter about a uniform or dress code?

❍ Did you answer the four questions in the Write Section on page 40?

❍ Did you use descriptive adjectives to describe the uniform or dress code?

❍ Did you use *will*?

❍ Did you use vocabulary from the unit?

ALTERNATIVE WRITING TOPICS

Write about one of the topics. Use the vocabulary and grammar from the unit.

1. Find a picture of a person in a magazine. Describe what that person has on. Does the person look good? Explain why or why not.

2. Is there a school or work uniform you like? Who wears it? Describe it. Why do you like it?

3. Think of a special place you will be going to soon. Describe what you will wear. Explain your answer.

RESEARCH TOPICS, see page 218.

UNIT 3 Art for Everyone

(1) FOCUS ON THE TOPIC

(A) PREDICT

Look at the picture. Discuss the questions with the class.

1. What is the man doing? *Hes is drawing.*
2. Where is he? *He's in a station.*
3. Do you know this man? *No I don't*

43

Work with a partner. Look at the two pictures. Fill in the chart. Then share your answers with the class.

Picture 1

Picture 2

	PICTURE 1	PICTURE 2
1. What do you see in each picture?	I see hands heart stomak numbers	I see beby
2. Give each picture a name or title.	I named it The deat under opration	beby is try
3. Which picture is more interesting to you?		✓

1 *Read the words and their definitions.*

an ad

ad /æd/ *noun.* short for *advertisement*; words or pictures that make you want to buy something

a drawing

drawing /ˈdrɔ ɪŋ/ *noun.* a picture made with a pencil, pen, or chalk[1]

energetic /ˌɛn ərˈdʒɛt ɪk/ *adjective.* very active

famous /ˈfeɪ məs/ *adjective.* known by a lot of people

graffiti

graffiti /grəˈfi ti/ *noun.* pictures and writing made on public walls and buildings

---

[1] **chalk:** Teachers use chalk to write on the blackboard.

museum /myu'zi əm/ *noun.* a place to look at (not to buy) art

painting /'pəɪn tɪŋ/ *noun.* a picture made with paint

a painting

public /'pʌb lɪk/ *adjective.* for everyone to see or use

sculpture /'skʌlp t ʃər/ *noun.* art made with wood, stone, or metal

a sculpture

2 *Complete each sentence with one of the words. You may need to use the plural form.*

1. Keith Haring liked to work and play a lot. He was very _____energetic_____.

2. Picasso and Rembrandt are more ___energetic___ than Keith Haring.

3. Today, people can see Haring's art in ___museums___ in the U.S., Japan, Brazil, and Europe.

4. Haring also made ___paints ads___ to sell things in magazines.

5. In the early 1980s, Haring made a lot of ___public___ art on the streets of New York. He wanted everyone to see his art.

6. When he made a ___paints drawing___, Haring used different colored pens, pencils, and chalk.

7. Leonardo da Vinci's *Mona Lisa* is a ___painting___ .

8. Michelangelo's *David* is a very famous ___sculpture___ . Usually Haring called his pieces *Untitled*.

9. Haring put ___graffiti___ on the walls of buildings and subways in New York City.

②FOCUS ON READING

Ⓐ READING ONE: Art for Everyone

1 *You are going to read a magazine interview. Before reading the interview, read the timeline about Keith Haring's life. Then answer the question on page 48.*

May 4, 1958	Haring is born in Kutztown, Pennsylvania.
1978	Haring goes to New York City. He studies at the School of Visual Arts. He draws graffiti in the NYC subway.
1979	Haring leaves the School of Visual Arts.
1981	He is arrested by the NYC police for drawing in the subway.
1982	He stops making graffiti. He has an art show at the Tony Shafrazi Gallery in NYC.
1983–1987	Haring works in Europe, Asia, and the USA.
1986	He paints a picture on the Berlin Wall in Germany. He opens the Pop Shop in NYC to sell his art.
1988	He opens the Pop Shop in Tokyo, Japan.
1989	Haring starts The Keith Haring Foundation to help children and people with AIDS.
February 16, 1990	He dies of AIDS.

What people, places, things, and ideas were important to Keith Haring?
Complete the chart.

PEOPLE	PLACES	THINGS	IDEAS / ACTIVITIES
people with AIDS			

2 Read the interview. Art World Magazine (AW) talked to Edwin T. Ramoran (ER) about the artist, Keith Haring. Mr. Ramoran is from the Bronx Museum of the Arts in New York.

ART FOR EVERYONE

1 **AW:** Mr. Ramoran, what kind of person was Keith Haring?

ER: Haring liked people. He liked parties and dancing. He was very **energetic**. You can see his energy in his art. His art moves and dances, too.

2 **AW:** When did Haring become **famous**?

ER: In 1978, he started to make pictures in the New York City subway. Some people were very upset. They said, "That isn't art. It's **graffiti**!"

3 But graffiti *is* art. And some people liked his art very much. They started to buy his **drawings, paintings**, and **sculptures**. Then galleries[1] became interested in his art,

too. By the mid-1980s, Keith Haring was famous around the world.

4 **AW:** What is Haring's art about? What does it mean?

ER: When people asked Haring, "What is your art about?" he answered, "You decide." His art is funny, energetic, and sometimes angry. It is also political.

5 His art is about education, freedom, and AIDS. These social issues were very important to Haring. His art is also about children. He worked with kids on many projects. For example, he made a large sculpture for a children's hospital in New York.

---

[1] **gallery:** a place to look at and buy art

6 **AW:** Was Haring different from other artists?

ER: Yes, he was.

7 **AW:** How was he different?

ER: Haring liked to make art in **public** places, like in the subway. He believed "art is for everyone." First, he was famous for his public art. Later, he became famous in galleries and **museums**.

8 He was also different because magazines had ads with his paintings and drawings. His drawings were also on other things, such as Swatch watches. He also sold his art in the Pop Shop. He used his art in unusual ways to communicate with the world.

9 **AW:** Is his art still popular?

ER: Yes, it is. Haring died in 1990, but people still feel his energy in his art. Today, we can see his art all around the world. Some of the money from his art helps AIDS organizations and children's organizations. His art still helps people. And if people want to learn more they can go to www.haring.com.

10 **AW:** Very interesting. Thank you, Mr. Ramoran.

ER: It was my pleasure.

◀ **READ FOR MAIN IDEAS**

Read each sentence. Circle the correct answer to complete the sentence.

1. In the early 1980s, Haring's art was in the _____ of New York City.
   a. subways
   b. galleries

2. Edwin Ramoran thinks that Haring made art for _____.
   a. money
   b. people

3. Haring's art was about _____.
   a. social issues
   b. famous people

Complete the sentences with the words from the box. Use each word only once.

ads   decide   energy   graffiti   money   public   social issues

1. You can see his _____energy_____ in his art.
2. Some people said his work was just _____graffiti_____ and not really art.
3. He was famous for his _____public_____ art first.
4. He made _____ads_____ for magazines.
5. People asked, "What is your art about?" Haring answered, "You _____decide_____."
6. _____Social issues_____, like AIDS and freedom, were important to Haring.
7. Some of the _____money_____ from the Pop Shop helped AIDS organizations and children's organizations.

◖ **MAKE INFERENCES**

Work with a partner. Why did people like Keith Haring's work? Check (✓) the two most important reasons. Then share your ideas with the class.

In the 1980s, people liked Haring's art because it was _____.

_____ different

_____ easy to understand

_____ energetic

_____ happy

_____ new

_____ public

_____ young

_____ your idea: _____

Give your opinion. Complete one sentence or both. Add you own ideas. Then share your opinion with the class.

I like Keith Haring's art because it is ___beatful___

___

I don't like Haring's art because it is ___not sweet___

___

B READING TWO: Look at Haring's Art

1 *Read the paragraph.*

Some of Keith Haring's art was just for fun. Other pieces were about social or political issues. In 1989 Haring made *Stop AIDS*. The snake is AIDS. The scissors are people working together to stop AIDS. In 1985 he made 20,000 *Free South Africa* posters. He wanted to help people in that country fight for freedom.

FREE SOUTH AFRICA

STOP AIDS

K. Haring®

2 *Each sentence is false. Change the underlined word to make it true.*

1. <u>All</u> of Keith Haring's art was just for fun. *Some*

2. The <u>scissors</u> in *Stop AIDS* symbolizes AIDS. *Snake*

3. Haring designed 20,000 <u>paintings</u> for people in South Africa in 1985. *Posters*

C INTEGRATE READINGS ONE AND TWO

◀ **STEP 1: Organize**

Look at all of the Haring pictures in this unit again. What important ideas are in Haring's art? Check (✓) the boxes. Then share your answers with the class.

IDEAS IN HARING'S ART	UNTITLED, 1984	RADIANT BABY	STOP AIDS	FREE SOUTH AFRICA
Politics				✓
AIDS			✓	
Love				
Energy	✓			
Freedom				✓
Children		✓		
_____ (other)				

◀ **STEP 2: Synthesize**

Use the chart in Organize to complete the sentences. Use each item only once.

1. ___RADIANT BABY___ is about ___Children___ and hope for the future.
   (Picture)   (Idea)
   There are rays around the child—like the rays of the sun. This shows the
   ___Energy___ of the child.
   (Idea)

2. ___Stop AIDS___ shows how people can work together to end a serious
   (Picture)
   problem such as ___AIDS___.
                    (Idea)

3. ___FREE South Africa___ is about ___Politics___. This picture is about the
   (Picture)   (Idea)
   fight for ___Freedom___.
             (Idea)

4. In ___UNTITLED___ you see a person. The person's arms go through his
      (Picture)
   heart and brain. This picture shows how ___Love___ is difficult.
                                            (Idea)

3 FOCUS ON WRITING

A VOCABULARY

◀ **REVIEW**

Complete the crossword puzzle with the words from the box.

| ads |
| art |
| different |
| drawings |
| energy |
| famous |
| galleries |
| graffiti |
| painter |
| pop |
| ~~public~~ |
| ~~shop~~ |
| social |

Across

1. In 1988, Haring opened the Pop _____ in Tokyo. It closed in 1989.

6. He believed "_____ is for everyone."

8. The word _____ is short for "popular."

9. Some people said, "This is not art. It's just _____."

10. _____ issues were very important to Haring.

11. Haring had a lot of _____. You can see it in his art. It "moves."

12. The word _____ is short for "advertisements."

Down

2. Haring made _____ art. He wanted everyone to see it.

3. People around the world know Haring. He is a _____ artist.

4. Someone who draws makes _____.

5. Haring was _____ from other artists.

7. A person who paints is a _____.

9. By the mid-1980s, Haring's work was in many art _____ around the world.

1 *Study the charts. The vocabulary for the unit is boldfaced.*

NOUNS	ADJECTIVES	VERBS
dance dancer dancing	x	dance
drawing	x	draw
energy	energetic	energize
freedom	free	free
paint **painting** painter	x	paint
politics politician	political	x
the public	**public**	publicize
sculpture sculptor sculpting	x	sculpt

A **noun** names: 　a **person** (an artist, Pablo Picasso) 　a **place** (a museum, London) 　a **thing** (a drawing) 　an **idea** (freedom) or **activity** (dancing) Nouns for people end in *-ist, -er, -or,* or *-ian.* *Painting* and *drawing* have two meanings. One is a thing (count noun), and one is an activity (non-count).	A **person** who paints is called a **painter** or **artist**. But a person who draws is only called an **artist**. Thing:　The *Mona Lisa* is a famous painting. My son made a drawing in art class. Activity:　Painting is a popular hobby. She likes drawing pictures in art class.
An **adjective** describes a noun. Some adjectives, like *energetic, artistic,* and *public,* end in *-ic.*	a **large** picture a **famous** person
Most **verbs** show action. Other verbs, like *be, have,* and *like,* do not show action.	Sofia **paints** very well. She **draws** well, too. Sofia **is** from Australia. She **has** a sister and a brother. She **likes** to practice yoga.

2　*Complete the sentences with the correct form of the words.*

　　1. (dance / dancing / dancer)

　　　　The tango is a ___dance___ from Argentina.

　　　　Julio Bocca is a famous tango ___dancer___ from Argentina.

　　　　Bocca's ___dancing___ is beautiful.

　　2. (draw / drawing)

　　　　This is a good ___drawing___ of my father. It looks like him.

　　　　We ___draw___ every day in art class.

　　　　Children enjoy ___drawing___ in school.

(continued on next page)

3. **(energetic / energy / energize)**

   Patrick is too tired to dance. He has no ___energy___.

   A cup of coffee will ___energize___ him.

   If he sleeps well tonight, he will be more ___energetic___ tomorrow.

4. **(free / freedom)**

   In this country, people are ___free___ to say almost anything.

   Not every country has this ___freedom___.

5. **(paint / painter / painting)**

   I have to buy more ___paint___ at the art store.

   I want to finish this ___painting___. It's a picture of my house.

   ___Painting___ is a fun activity.

   I'm a good ___painter___.

6. **(political / politics)**

   I am not interested in ___politics___.

   My teacher's ideas are very ___political___.

7. **(public / the public / publicize)**

   ___The Public___ likes the new show at the Shafrazi Gallery.

   They ___publicize___ the big art shows on TV and in newspapers.

   Mila likes to go to ___public___ places like parks and malls.

8. **(sculptor / sculpture / sculpting)**

   Constantin Brancusi is a famous ___sculptor___.

   ___Sculpting___ was one way he made art.

   The Kiss is a ___sculpture___ by Brancusi.

◖ CREATE

Write three more sentences about Keith Haring and his art. Use one word from the chart on page 54 in each sentence.

1. _____

2. _____

3. _____

B **GRAMMAR: Simple Past of *Be* and *Have***

1 *Read the excerpt from the interview about Keith Haring. Then answer the questions.*

AW: Was Haring different from other artists?
ER: Yes, he was.

AW How was he different?
ER: Haring liked to make art in public places, like in the subway. He believed "art is for everyone." First, he was famous for his public art. Later, he became famous in galleries and museums.

He was also different because magazines had ads with his paintings and drawings. His drawings were also on other things, such as Swatch watches. He also sold his art in the Pop Shop. He used his art in unusual ways to communicate with the world.

Underline *was, were,* and *had* in the interview. How many examples can you find?

was __5__   *were* __1__   *had* __1__

When do we use *am, is, are,* and *have*? __in present__ tense

When do we use *was, were,* and *had*? __in past tens__

THE SIMPLE PAST OF *BE*

1. The **simple past** forms of *be* are *was* and *were*.	Keith Haring **was** an artist. Social issues **were** important to him.

2. For negative sentences, use:
 	
   subject + *was* / *were* + *not*
 	
In speaking and informal writing, use:
 	
   wasn't* / *weren't
	His art **was not** in museums at first.
	
	His parents **were not** famous.
	
	His art **wasn't** in museums at first.
	
	His parents **weren't** famous.

3. For *yes / no* questions, use: ***was* / *were* + subject**	**Was Haring** different from other artists? **Were his drawings** popular? **Was Haring** famous in the 1970s?
4. For *Wh-* questions, use: ***Wh-* word + *was* / *were* + subject**	**Who was** Keith Haring? **What was** his art about? **How were** his pictures different?

SIMPLE PAST OF *HAVE*

1. The **simple past** form of *have* is *had*.	Haring **had** a lot of energy.

2. For negative sentences, use:
 	
   did* + *not* + *have
 	
In speaking and informal writing, use:
 	
   didn't have
	Haring **did not have** a brother.
	
	Haring **didn't have** a brother.

3. For *yes / no* questions, use: ***did* + subject + *have***	**Did Haring have** fun with his art? **Did Haring have** a long career?
4. For *Wh-* questions, use: ***Wh-* word + *did* + subject + *have***	**Where did Haring have** fun? **When did Haring have** the most success?

How

2 Complete each sentence with **was, wasn't, were, weren't, had,** or **didn't have**.

1. Keith Haring and Andy Warhol ___were___ famous artists in the 1980s.

2. Both Haring and Warhol _were_ from Pennsylvania, but they _were_ from different cities.

3. Haring and Warhol (not) _weren't_ the same age. Warhol _was_ 31 years older than Haring.

4. Warhol and Haring _didn't have_ a lot of friends.

5. Warhol _was_ a student at the Carnegie Institute of Technology.

6. In the 1950s, Warhol _had_ a job on Madison Avenue in New York.

7. He _was_ an artist for *Vogue* and *Glamour* magazines.

8. He (not) _didn't have_ a lot of money at that time.

9. By the early 1960s, Andy Warhol _was_ a famous Pop artist.

10. Like Haring's art, Warhol's art _was_ controversial.

11. Warhol _was_ a painter, sculptor, writer, and filmmaker.

12. Keith Haring _was_ a painter and a sculptor, but he (not) _wasn't_ a writer or a filmmaker.

13. Warhol and Haring _were_ good friends in the 1980s.

14. Haring _was_ very sad when Warhol died in 1987.

15. Warhol _was_ 58 years old when he died.

16. He (not) _didn't have_ a very long life.

3 Work with a partner. Write questions about Keith Haring and his art. Use the past forms of **be** and **have**.

1. Who / be / Keith Haring?   Who was Keith Haring?

2. Be / Haring / famous in the 1970s? Was Haring famous in the 1970s?

3. Be / Keith Haring / energetic? Was Keith Haring energetic?

4. In what city / be / Haring / born? In what city was born?

5. Be / Haring / only a painter? Was Haring only a painter?

6. Why / be / his art / controversial? Why was his art controversial?

7. Be / the Pop Shop / a restaurant? Was the Pop shop a restaurant?

8. Where / be / the two Pop Shops? Where were the two Pop shops?

9. How old / be / Keith Haring / in 1990? How Old was Keith Haring in 1990?

4 Give your book to your partner. Your partner will write answers to your questions in full sentences.

Your partner's answers:

was born ✓

1. Keith Haring was an artist in the 1980s.

2. Yes, he was.

3. Yes, he was.

4. He borned in Kutztown in Pennsylvania

5. No, he wasn't only Pinter.

6. _____

7. No, it wasn't

8. _____

9. _____

In this unit, you read a timeline and an interview about Keith Haring. You also looked at examples of Keith Haring's art.

You are going to **write a biography about Keith Haring.** A **biography** is a story of a person's life. Use the vocabulary and grammar from the unit.*

◀ PREPARE TO WRITE: Finding Information in a Reading

To help you plan your biography, you are going to **look for information in the readings** in this unit as a prewriting activity.

1 *Look at the timeline on page 47. Then answer the questions about Keith Haring.*

1. Where was Keith Haring born?

   Keith Haring was born in Kutztown, Pennsylvania.

2. When was Keith Haring born?

3. When was Haring arrested by the police? Why?

4. When and where was Haring an art student?

5. What were his first drawings? Where were they?

6. When and where was Haring's first important art show?

2 *Look at Reading One on pages 48–49. Find one more idea about Keith Haring that you think is interesting. Write it on the line. Use this information in your biography, too.*

---

*For Alternative Writing Topics, see page 64. These topics can be used in place of the writing topic for this unit or as homework. The alternative topics relate to the theme of the unit, but may not target the same grammar or rhetorical structures taught in the unit.

WRITE: Time Order

A biography usually gives events in **time order** (the order they happened). The writer begins with the first event and ends with the last event.

1 *Read the sentences about Andy Warhol. Number the sentences in time order from 1 to 7.*

_____ **a.** Warhol was a student at Carnegie Institute of Technology from 1945 to 1949.

_____ **b.** Andy Warhol and Keith Haring were good friends in the 1980s.

_____ **c.** Andy Warhol died in 1987.

_____ **d.** By the early 1960s, Andy Warhol was a famous Pop artist.

__1__ **e.** Andy Warhol was born in Pennsylvania in 1912.

_____ **f.** In the 1950s, Warhol was a commercial[1] artist on Madison Avenue in New York.

_____ **g.** Warhol had his first art show in 1952.

2 *Work with a partner. Compare your answers for Exercise 1. Were your answers the same as your partner's? Talk about any differences.*

3 *Look at your answers to the questions about Keith Haring in Prepare to Write on page 61. Put them in time order.*

4 *Write your first draft. Include a topic sentence that gives the main idea of your paragraph. Write sentences to explain or support the main idea. Don't worry about grammar yet. Just try to make your ideas clear.*

REVISE: Using Commas in Dates and the Names of Places

1 *Study the examples. Notice where the commas are.*

1. Keith Haring was born on May 4, 1958.

2. Keith Haring was born on Monday, May 4, 1958.

3. Haring was born in May of 1958.

4. He was born in 1958.

5. The Harings were from Kutztown, Pennsylvania.

6. The Harings were from Kutztown.

---

[1] **commercial:** for business or money

7. They lived in Kutztown, Pennsylvania, in the 1970s.

8. Haring visited Madrid, Spain.

9. Haring visited Spain many times.

10. Haring visited Madrid, Spain, many times.

Use a comma:
- In complete dates (#s 1, 2)
- After a city name if the state (or country) name is next (#s 5, 7, 8, 10)
- After the city *and* state (or country) name *if* there are more words after the state/country (#s 7, 10)

2 *Add commas to the sentences. Not every sentence needs commas.*

1. Haring was born on May 4, 1958.

2. Haring moved to New York, New York in 1978.

3. He had his first important show in 1982.

4. Haring opened the Pop Shop in New York City in 1986. It closed in September of 1995.

5. The Pop Shop in Tokyo, Japan opened on January 30, 1988. It closed in 1989.

6. Keith Haring was in Pisa Italy on Sunday, June 19, 1989.

7. Haring died on Friday February 16, 1990.

3 *Write three sentences about yourself (for example, your address or your birthday). Use commas with dates and the names of places.*

1. I was born on septembe 2nd, 1980.

2. I got marrid on may 15th, 2014.

3. I was in Tarhun, Libya in 1999.

◀ **EDIT: Writing the Final Draft**

Prepare to write the final draft of your biography. Check your grammar, spelling, capitalization, and punctuation. Check that you used some of the vocabulary and grammar from the unit. Use the checklist to help you write your final draft. Then neatly write or type your biography.

✓ FINAL DRAFT CHECKLIST

○ Did you use a capital letter at the beginning of each sentence?
○ Did you use a period at the end of each sentence?
○ Did you use commas in the correct places?
○ Did you put the events in time order?
○ Did you use the past forms of *be* and *have*?
○ Did you use vocabulary from the unit?

ALTERNATIVE WRITING TOPICS

Write about one of the topics. Use the vocabulary and grammar from the unit.

1. Look at the pictures on pages 43, 44, and 51 again. Choose one picture. Write five to ten sentences about this picture. What is it? How does it make you feel?

2. Keith Haring used simple symbols (such as babies, dogs, and dancers) that were important to the people in the 1970s and 1980s. What symbols are important to people today? Draw one. Write five to ten sentences about your symbol.

3. Keith Haring wanted everyone to experience his art. It was "art for everyone." What do you think? Was Haring's art "for everyone"? Write five to ten sentences.

4. Haring's art was controversial, especially in the 1980s. Some people liked it, and some people didn't like it. Look at the pictures on pages 43, 44, and 51 again. Why do you think Haring's art was controversial? Write five to ten sentences about Haring and his art.

RESEARCH TOPICS, see page 219.

What's It Worth to You?

①FOCUS ON THE TOPIC

A PREDICT

Look at the picture. Discuss the questions with the class.

1. What does the man have?

2. What is the woman saying?

3. Why does the man look so happy?

65

Picture

Do you have a special possession: a photo or your grandmother's ring? Do you collect anything: stamps, dolls, or coins? Write your special possession or collection in the chart. Then ask three classmates about their special possessions or collections. Write their answers.

NAME	POSSESSION / COLLECTION	WHY DO YOU HAVE IT?
You	old coins	to Remember
Student 1	Salm's grand father's picture	to
Student 2	a Hand strap	his sister gave him
Student 3	a cell phone	because he wants call his friend

C **BACKGROUND** AND **VOCABULARY**

Read the passage. Then write the boldfaced word next to its definition on the next page. Compare your answers with a partner's.

unusual

Antiques Roadshow is a popular television show. The show travels to different cities. The **guests** are regular people. They bring their special possessions to the show. They tell stories and ask questions.

The guests bring many kinds of **items**. Some guests bring antiques—old and **valuable** things, such as art, furniture, or jewelry. Some items are very common and are not worth a lot of money. But others are very rare and valuable. Some of the items are in very bad **condition**, but others are in great condition—just like new. Some items have only **sentimental** value—maybe the item was a gift from someone special or brings back good memories.

Antiques **experts** give information about the items. The experts also say how much the items are worth. The guests always want to know the value of their items.

People can learn a lot on this show. It is very **educational**. This type of TV show started in England more than 20 years ago. You can see similar shows in other countries around the world.

experts	1. people with a lot of knowledge and experience with something
guests	2. people who visit a person or place
sentimental	3. having a value in personal feelings or emotions
educational	4. helping you to learn
rare	5. not common; not often seen
items	6. objects or things
condition	7. the physical state of something—good or bad
valuable	8. having a high price, worth a lot of money

2 FOCUS ON READING

A READING ONE: My Secret[1]

1 *Dan Stone writes a sports column for the* Boston Daily News. *Read the beginning of the sports column. Then, with a partner, answer the question: What is Dan Stone's secret?*

My Secret
_____ By Dan Stone

I am a sports writer, and I love my job because I love sports, especially football and basketball. But I have a secret.

Every Monday night I watch my favorite TV show. If the telephone rings, I don't answer it. I tell my friends that I am watching *Monday Night Football*, but that isn't true.

---

[1] **secret:** information that you don't tell other people

My Secret
By Dan Stone

1 I am a sports writer, and I love my job because I love sports, especially football and basketball. But I have a secret.

2 Every Monday night I watch my **favorite** TV show. If the telephone rings, I don't answer it. I tell my friends that I am watching *Monday Night Football*, but that isn't true.

3 My favorite show is more exciting than *Monday Night Football*. It is also very **educational**. I learn a lot about art and **history** every week.

4 Here is my secret: On Monday nights I watch *Antiques Roadshow*. It is a show about antiques and **collections**. It's great! Fourteen million people watch it every week.

5 The show is simple. The **guests** on the show are real people. The guests bring in old art, furniture, books, toys, and much, much more. First, the guests tell the **experts** about their **items**. The stories are the best part of *Roadshow*. Then the experts talk about the items. Finally, the experts say how much the items are **worth**.

6 One woman, Veronica, had a painting with trees and animals in it. Veronica's grandmother got the picture for free in 1925. The expert looked at Veronica's picture carefully and said, "This is very **rare**. Thomas Cole is the artist. Cole painted this around 1835. Your painting is worth about $125,000." Veronica was very surprised. She told the expert, "Wow! That's a lot of money! But I don't care about the money. I'm going to keep it. The painting has a lot of **sentimental** value."

7 I want *Antiques Roadshow* to visit my city. I can't wait! I have a baseball signed by Babe Ruth and Jackie Robinson in the 1940s. It's in perfect **condition**. I also have a baseball card collection. I keep it in a box under my bed. The ball and the cards have sentimental value. My father gave them to me. But I don't really like to play or watch baseball. Maybe they are worth a lot of money!

8 And you? Are you ready? Look carefully around your home! You might have something very **valuable**.

9 So, remember, don't call me on Monday nights. I'm watching "football."

READ FOR MAIN IDEAS

*Read each sentence. Check (✓) **True** or **False**. Then write the number of the paragraph where you found the answer.*

	True	False	Paragraph Number
1. People who watch *Antiques Roadshow* can learn a lot.	✓	○	3
2. Dan Stone watches football on Monday nights.	○	✓	2, 4
3. *Antiques Roadshow* is a sports show.	○	✓	4
4. *Antiques Roadshow* buys items from the guests.	✓	○	5

READ FOR DETAILS

Match each question to the correct answer. Then write the number of the paragraph where you found the answer.

__e (2)__ **1.** What do Stone's friends think he watches on Monday nights?

__c__ **2.** What do people learn about on *Antiques Roadshow*?

__a (5)__ **3.** What do people bring to *Antiques Roadshow*?

__d__ **4.** For Stone, what is the best part of the show?

__b__ **5.** How much is the woman's picture worth?

__c__ **6.** What does Stone want to bring to *Antiques Roadshow*?

a. items from home

b. $125,000

c. art and history

d. the stories

e. football

f. an autographed baseball and his baseball cards

MAKE INFERENCES

*Read each sentence. Write **T** (true) or **F** (false). Share your answers with a partner.*

_____ **1.** Dan Stone likes antiques more than sports.

__F__ **2.** Most people sell their items if they are valuable.

__F__ **3.** Dan Stone wants to sell his baseball cards.

__F__ **4.** Dan's friends will laugh at him if they learn his secret.

In his article Dan Stone said, "Fourteen million people watch it every week." Why is Antiques Roadshow *popular? Check (✓) all the possible answers. Then share your answers with the class.*

Antiques Roadshow is popular because _____.

____✓ **1.** the show is educational

____✓ **2.** people need money

_____ **3.** the people on the show are funny

____✓ **4.** people remember their family history

____✓ **5.** the stories are interesting

____✓ **6.** the guests are real people

_____ **7.** your idea: _____

B READING TWO: Be a Smart Collector

1 *Read the rules from an expert about collecting.*

BE A SMART COLLECTOR

Starting a collection is easy, but be a smart collector. Here are four rules:

RULE 1: Enjoy. Collect things that you are interested in. Collect things that you want to keep for a long time.

RULE 2: Learn. Become an expert. Read a lot. Talk to antiques experts. Ask a lot of questions. Don't worry! Experts love to talk.

RULE 3: Look for the best. Collect things in good condition. For example, an antique toy in "mint," or perfect, condition will be valuable in the future. A similar toy in bad condition will not be as valuable.

RULE 4: Buy rare items. Collect items that are rare. Rare things are more valuable than common things. If the items you collect are rare today, they will be more valuable in the future.

2 Match each example with one of the rules on page 70. Write the rule number
(**1, 2, 3,** or **4**) on the line.

_2_ **a.** First, learn about antique toys. Then collect them.

_4_ **b.** Collecting coins from the 1800s is better than collecting common
coins from today.

_1_ **c.** If you love Barbie® dolls, then collect them.

_3_ **d.** Don't buy a stamp for your collection if it is ripped.

**A ripped
stamp**

C INTEGRATE READINGS ONE AND TWO

◖ **STEP 1: Organize**

_Read Dan Stone's letter again. Does Dan follow the four rules? Write ideas
about Dan's collection in the boxes._

	IDEAS FROM DAN STONE'S LETTER
Rule 1: Enjoy	Dan doesn't like baseball, but his collection has sentimental value.
Rule 2: Learn	
Rule 3: Look for the best	
Rule 4: Buy rare items	

◖ **STEP 2: Synthesize**

_Dan Stone has a collection of baseball items. Is Dan Stone a smart collector?
Did he follow the four rules? Complete the first sentence. Then write 4–5 more
sentences to explain._

Dan Stone (is / isn't) a smart collector. He _____

_____

_____

_____

_____

3 FOCUS ON WRITING

A VOCABULARY

◖ REVIEW

Complete the sentences with the correct words.

1. (**condition** / **valuable**)

   I found some of my childhood toys in my mother's house. Maybe they

   are ___valuable___ today. They are all in good ___condition___ .

2. (**antique** / **worth**)

   My mother collects ___antique___ jewelry. She has a very old watch.

   The watch isn't ___worth___ very much, but she enjoys wearing it.

3. (**collection** / **collector** / **collect**)

   I began to ___collect___ stamps when I was ten years old. I plan to

   give my ___collection___ to my son when he is ten years old. I hope he

   wants to be a stamp ___collector___ , like me.

4. (**sentimental** / **rare**)

   This was my grandparents' kitchen table. You can't buy a table like it

   today. It is very ___rare___ . It isn't a beautiful table, but I keep it

   because it has a lot of ___sentimental___ value.

5. (**expert** / **favorite** / **history**)

   My father likes to read about ___history___ . His ___favorite___

   subject is the U.S. Civil War. He is an ___expert___ on the Civil

   War. He knows a lot about it.

Remember that a **noun** is a person, place, thing, or idea. An **adjective** is a word that describes a noun. A **verb** shows an action.

Some nouns end in *-tion, -ment,* and *-or.* Some adjectives end in *-ing, -ed, -al, -able,* and *-ible.*

Some words like *expert* and *sports* are both a noun and an adjective.

Work with a partner. Put the words into the correct group.

~~collect~~	condition	excite	expert	valuable
collectible	educate	excited	possession	value
collection	education	excitement	sentimental	
collector	educational	exciting	sports	

NOUNS	ADJECTIVES	VERBS
condition collectible educate education excitement collector excitement value	expert valuabale sentimental educational exciting excited	collect excite educat

◖ CREATE

Write your special possession or collection on the first line. Then write sentences about it. Use one word from Expand in each sentence.

My special possession/collection . . .

1.   My special possession is a watch. It is valuable.
2.   I have a valuabal phone.
3.   I ecite with my phone.
4.   My phone is sentimental.
5.   We are English language collectors.

1 *Read the excerpt from "My Secret." Then answer the questions.*

> I am a sports writer, and I love my job because I love sports, especially football and basketball. But I have a secret.
>
> Every Monday night I watch my favorite TV show. If the telephone rings, I don't answer it. I tell my friends that I am watching *Monday Night Football*, but that isn't true.

1. How many verbs are there? Underline them.

2. Which verbs are negative? Circle them.

3. These sentences are about ____.
   a. the past
   b. the present
   c. the future

THE SIMPLE PRESENT	
1. Use the **simple present tense** for everyday actions or facts.	I **have** a secret. If the telephone **rings**, I **don't answer** it.
2. When the subject is *he, she,* or *it*, put an *s* at the end of the regular verbs. REMEMBER: *be* and *have* are irregular.	She collect**s** antique jewelry. *Antiques Roadshow* **is** my favorite show. Dan **has** a secret.
3. For negative sentences, use: ***do* (or *does*) + *not* + the base form of the verb** Use the contractions ***don't*** and ***doesn't*** in speaking and informal writing.	Stone **does not watch** football on Mondays. I **do not like** to play golf. If the telephone rings, I **don't** answer it.
4. For *yes / no* questions, use: ***Do* (or *Does*) + subject + the base form of the verb** Use *do* or *does* in short answers.	**Do diamonds cost** a lot? **Yes, they do.** **Does Dan Stone watch** football on Mondays? **No, he doesn't.**

5. For *wh-* questions, use:	**What do you watch** on Monday nights?
***Wh-* word + *do* (or *does*) + subject + the base form of the verb**	**Where do you like** to play golf? **How much does that car cost?**

2 *Complete the conversation with the present tense form of each verb.*

EXPERT: Welcome to *Antiques Roadshow*. What _____ do _____ you

_____ have _____ with you today?
1. (have)

WOMAN: I _____ have _____ my mother's diamond wedding ring. I love
2. (have)

this ring very much. I _____ remember _____ my mother when I
3. (remember)

_____ wear _____ it.
4. (wear)

EXPERT: _____ Do _____ you _____ wear _____ it often?
5. (wear)

WOMAN: Yes, I _____ do _____. I never _____ take _____ it off.
6. (do)   7. (take)

EXPERT: What _____ Do _____ you _____ know _____ about this ring?
8. (know)

WOMAN: My father gave it to my mother in 1964. I _____ don't know _____ where he
9. (not / know)

got it. My husband _____ doesn't think _____ that it _____ is _____ worth a lot
10. (not / think)   11. (be)

of money. _____ Does _____ it _____ look _____ valuable to you?
12. (look)

EXPERT: Well, it _____ is _____ a beautiful ring, but I have some bad news.
13. (be)

This _____ isn't _____ a real diamond. It _____ is _____ fake. It is
14. (not / be)   15. (be)

worth about $50.

WOMAN: Really? My husband was right! Well, I still _____ love _____ it. My
16. (love)

husband and I _____ plan _____ to give it to our daughter. We
17. (plan)

_____ want _____ this ring to stay in our family. It _____ has _____ a lot
18. (want)   19. (have)

of sentimental value. Thank you very much!

In this unit, you read about special possessions and collections.

You are going to **write a paragraph about your own special possession or collection**. Use the vocabulary and grammar and from the unit.*

◀ **PREPARE TO WRITE: Questioning Yourself**

To get ideas for your writing, you are going to **ask yourself questions** about a topic. For example: Do I have a special possession or collection? What is it? Why do I keep it? Was it a gift? Does it have sentimental value? Is it worth a lot of money?

1 *Think of some special possessions or collections that you have. Make a list of four or five items. A special possession can be something that:*

- you collect.
- you received as a gift.
- helps you remember a special person, event, or time in your life.

Example

My Special Possessions:

my high school soccer shirt   my grandfather's painting
family photos

2 *Choose two special possessions from the list you made. Complete the chart.*

	POSSESSION 1	**POSSESSION 2**
1. What is your special possession?		
2. Where did you get it?		
3. How much is it worth?		
4. Why do you keep it?		

---

*For Alternative Writing Topics, see page 81. These topics can be used in place of the writing topic for this unit or as homework. The alternative topics relate to the theme of the unit, but may not target the same grammar or rhetorical structures taught in the unit.

3 *Choose one possession to write about.*

◖ **WRITE: A Paragraph**

A **paragraph** is a group of sentences about one main idea. The first sentence usually gives the main idea of the paragraph. It is called the topic sentence. The other sentences explain or support the topic sentence.

1 *Read the paragraph. Then answer the questions.*

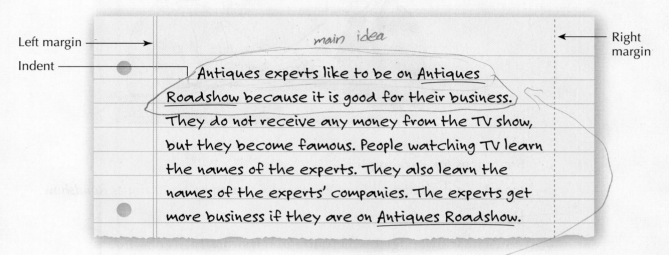

Left margin →

Right margin ←

Indent →

main idea

Antiques experts like to be on Antiques Roadshow because it is good for their business. They do not receive any money from the TV show, but they become famous. People watching TV learn the names of the experts. They also learn the names of the experts' companies. The experts get more business if they are on Antiques Roadshow.

1. What is the main idea of this paragraph? Circle the sentence that has the main idea.

2. Does the writer begin each new sentence on a new line, or does the writer <u>continue on the same line</u>?

3. When does the writer stop and move down to the next line?

when a paragraph finshed.

2 *Write two paragraphs with these sentences on a separate piece of paper. The sentences are in the correct order. Follow the rules for paragraph form. Your paragraphs will look like the paragraph on page 77.*

Sentences for Paragraph 1

One day, a man named Russ Pritchard was a guest on *Antiques Roadshow*.

He had a large sword.

When he was young, Pritchard found the sword in his new house.

George Juno, an antiques expert, told Pritchard it was an American Civil War sword.

Juno said the sword was very rare and worth $35,000.

Pritchard was very surprised to hear this.

Sentences for Paragraph 2

Two years later, there was a story in the newspaper about Pritchard and Juno.

WGBH, a Boston TV station, learned that Pritchard's story was not true.

Pritchard and Juno made up the story together.

WGBH was very angry because it wants only true stories on *Antiques Roadshow*.

As a result, Juno cannot be on *Antiques Roadshow* in the future.

3 *Read the paragraph. Underline the topic sentence.*

> One of my special possessions is my collection of family photographs. I have hundreds of photos. I have very old photos of my great-grandparents. I also have pictures of my grandparents' wedding. I especially love the photos of my parents when they were children. Sometimes I spend hours looking at the pictures. I like the photos because my family is very important to me.

4 *Read the paragraph. It is missing a topic sentence. Read the topic sentences. Choose the best topic sentence and write it on the line.*

> _My high school soccer shirt is very important to me_. It is yellow and black and has the number "11" on it. It also has my name on the back. I got it in high school when I played on the school's team. Our team won every game. The shirt has a lot of sentimental value. I keep it because I like to remember those games and my teammates. We had a lot of fun together.

Topic Sentences

  a. My team won every game in high school.

  b. My high school soccer shirt is very important to me.

  c. Soccer is my favorite sport.

5 *Look back at Prepare to Write, Exercise 3, on page 77. What special possession are you going to write about? Write a topic sentence for your paragraph.*

6 *Write your first draft. Include a topic sentence that gives the main idea of your paragraph. Write sentences to explain or support the main idea. Don't worry about grammar yet. Just try to make your ideas clear.*

◖ **REVISE:** Staying on the Topic

All the sentences in a paragraph explain and support the main idea. Sentences about other ideas or topics do not belong. Read the paragraph. The topic sentence is underlined. One sentence is not about the main idea. It is crossed out.

> One of my special possessions is a painting by my grandfather. He was not a professional painter, but he painted as a hobby. ~~My sister also paints.~~ My favorite painting is a picture of the house where my father grew up. The house is yellow and there are trees around it. My grandfather gave me the picture before he died. I think of him when I look at the picture.

1 *Read the paragraph. Underline the topic sentence. Cross out one sentence that is not about the main idea. Work with a partner. Explain why you chose that sentence to cross out.*

> My bicycle is a very special possession. My bike is not worth a lot of money. It is old, but it is in good condition. I ride my bike every day. I ride it to school, to the store, and to my grandmother's house. ~~I walk to these places in the summer.~~ I can go wherever I want because I have a bike.

2 *Look at the first draft of your paragraph. Do all the sentences explain and support the topic sentence? Cross out the sentences that are not about the main idea. If necessary, write new sentences.*

◖ **EDIT:** Writing the Final Draft

Prepare to write the final draft of your paragraph. Check your grammar, spelling, capitalization, and punctuation. Check that you used some of the grammar and vocabulary from the unit. Use the checklist to help you write your final draft. Then neatly write or type your paragraph.

✔️ FINAL DRAFT CHECKLIST

- ○ Did you begin with a good topic sentence?
- ○ Did you use sentences to explain or support the topic sentence?
- ○ Did you use the correct form of simple present tense verbs?
- ○ Did you use vocabulary from the unit?

ALTERNATIVE WRITING TOPICS

Write about one of the topics. Use the vocabulary and grammar from the unit.

1. Ask someone what his or her favorite possession or collection is. Write a paragraph about the person's answer.

2. Why do people bring items to *Antiques Roadshow*? Are they interested in history and sentimental value? Are they interested in money? Write a paragraph with your opinion.

3. Is there a TV show like *Antiques Roadshow* in your country? If yes, write a paragraph about the show.

RESEARCH TOPICS, see page 220.

UNIT 5

Strength in Numbers

القوة في الجمع

1 FOCUS ON THE TOPIC

A PREDICT

Look at the picture. Discuss the questions with the class.

1. Who are the people?   Guardians

2. What are they wearing?   uniform

3. What do they do?

4. Look at the title. What does "Strength in Numbers" mean?

B SHARE INFORMATION

*Read the list of social issues. Are these problems for young people in your city or town? Rate each social issue from **1** (not a problem) to **4** (a serious problem). Circle the number. Discuss your answers with the class.*

SOCIAL ISSUES	Not a Problem			A Serious Problem
1. Alcohol	1	2	3	(4)
2. Drugs	1	2	3	(4)
3. Not finding a job	1	2	3	(4)
4. Gangs[1]	1	2	(3)	4
5. Having babies	1	2	3	(4)
6. Smoking	1	2	(3)	4
7. Not staying in school	1	2	(3)	4
8. Your idea _____ :	1	2	3	4

without marrige (handwritten note beside item 5)

C BACKGROUND AND VOCABULARY

1 *Read the information about the Guardian Angels.*

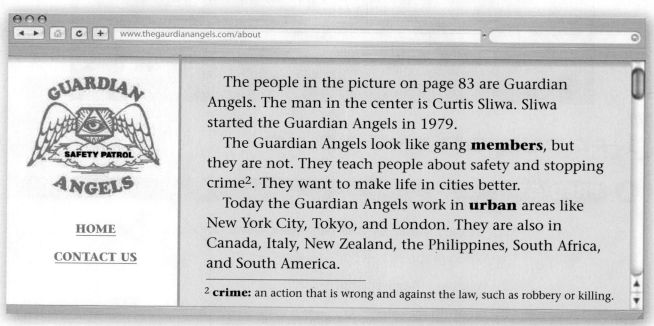

www.thegaurdianangels.com/about

GUARDIAN
SAFETY PATROL
ANGELS

HOME

CONTACT US

The people in the picture on page 83 are Guardian Angels. The man in the center is Curtis Sliwa. Sliwa started the Guardian Angels in 1979.

The Guardian Angels look like gang **members**, but they are not. They teach people about safety and stopping crime[2]. They want to make life in cities better.

Today the Guardian Angels work in **urban** areas like New York City, Tokyo, and London. They are also in Canada, Italy, New Zealand, the Philippines, South Africa, and South America.

[2] **crime:** an action that is wrong and against the law, such as robbery or killing.

[1] **gangs:** groups of young people who often make trouble

HOME

CONTACT US

The Guardian Angels have a special program called Urban Angels. The Urban Angels program **supports** teenagers in urban areas. Some **at-risk** teenagers need help to stay out of trouble. These teenagers can join the Urban Angels program and learn how to **avoid** drugs, gangs, and other problems. The program also teaches teens to **respect** older people. Older people can teach kids a lot.

The Guardian Angels want Urban Angels to be **positive** members of their communities. The Urban Angels clean up parks and help homeless people. They serve as **role models** for younger kids.

2 *Match the words on the left with the definitions on the right. Then read the passage on pages 84–85 again.*

_b_ **1.** members	**a.** stay away from
_g_ **2.** urban	**b.** people who are in a group, club, or organization
_f_ **3.** supports	**c.** good, helpful, not negative
_e_ **4.** at-risk	**d.** people who are good examples for other people to follow
_a_ **5.** avoid	**e.** may have problems in the future
_h_ **6.** respect	**f.** gives money, food, or help to someone
_c_ **7.** positive	**g.** big-city
_d_ **8.** role models	**h.** honor, have a good or high opinion of someone

win
won

A READING ONE: Urban Angels

1 *Read the chart. List the problems in order from the most common to the least common.*

SOCIAL ISSUES AND PROBLEMS FOR U.S.TEENAGERS	
Number of Teenagers Per Month	**Issue or Problem**
34,675	Start smoking
15,983	Arrested for drugs
223	Killed by guns
1,306	Hurt by guns
7,592	Arrested for violent crimes
35,925	Have babies

1. ___Have babies___
2. ___Start___
3. _____
4. _____
5. _____
6. ___Killed by guns___

2 *Read the brochure about the Urban Angels.*

URBAN ANGELS

A program to address important issues facing teenagers in the U.S.

Frequently Asked Questions about the Urban Angels

1 **What is the Urban Angels Life Skills Program?**

2 Urban Angels is a group, or club, for **teenagers**. The Guardian Angels started Urban Angels to **support at-risk** teens in the South Bronx in New York City. The Urban Angels Life Skills Program helps teens **avoid** drugs, gangs, guns, **crime**, and other trouble. The program wants teens to stay in school and to become **positive members** of their community.

3 **What do Urban Angels do?**

4 Urban Angels do many things. They have activities after school two days a week and two Saturdays a month. These activities are educational and fun.

5 Urban Angels go on trips to museums in New York City and to other places outside the city. They visit businesses to learn about different jobs. Most important, Urban Angels help out in their community. For example, Urban Angels paint over graffiti at neighborhood "paint-outs." At "park clean-ups" they go to city parks and make them beautiful again. They also have programs for feeding homeless people.

6 **What do Urban Angels learn?**

7 Urban Angels take special classes. In class, they learn about social issues. They also learn how to stop problems in their community. They learn to take care of themselves, their families, and their neighbors. These teenagers become **role models** for younger kids. Most important, Urban Angels learn to **respect** themselves. They learn that they are important members of their community.

Curtis Sliwa with award

Sliwa, "Rocky Pasta e fagioli," Mary "Gold Card" Sliwa, and Frances Sliwa, Curtis' mother

Guardian Angel K.C. and her daughter, Urban Angel Rosie

(continued on next page)

8 Why do Urban Angels have nicknames[1]?

9 Urban Angels have nicknames to show their personalities and their goals for the future. For example, one young man has the nickname "Bear." He likes his nickname because he is big like a bear. He also likes this nickname because bears are strong, but they take care of their families, too.

10 Can I become an Urban Angel?

11 Today, you can become an Urban Angel if you are a teenager from the South Bronx or Washington, D.C. In the future, there might be Urban Angel groups in other cities.

12 Who pays for the Urban Angels program?

13 The New York City government and generous people from New York and other cities support the Urban Angels program.

Graffiti paint-out

14 How can I help?

15 For more information and to learn how you can support the Urban Angels, write to us at:

16 The Alliance of the Guardian Angels
717 Fifth Avenue, Suite 401
New York, NY 10022 USA

---

[1] **nickname:** a special name or a short form of your real name

◖ **READ FOR MAIN IDEAS**

Check (✓) the true sentences.

The Urban Angels program . . .

_____ **1.** is for adults.

__✓__ **2.** helps its members feel good about themselves.

_____ **3.** finds jobs for its members.

__✓__ **4.** teaches its members about social issues.

__✓__ **5.** teaches young people about community service.

Complete the sentences. Match the phrases on the left with the phrases on the right.

_c_ **1.** The Guardian Angels . . .

_d_ **2.** The South Bronx . . .

_c_ **3.** The Urban Angels program . . .

_h_ **4.** Their nicknames . . .

_b_ **5.** On weekends and after school, Urban Angels . . .

_g_ **6.** Teens under 18 years of age who live in the South Bronx and Washington, D.C. . . .

_a_ **7.** The money for the program . . .

_e_ **8.** If you want to help the Urban Angels, you . . .

a. comes from the City of New York and from generous people.

b. go on "paint-outs" and "park clean-ups."

c. started the Urban Angels program.

d. is a neighborhood in New York City.

e. can write to the Guardian Angels for more information.

f. helps teens stay away from trouble.

g. can become Urban Angels.

h. show their personalities and goals.

◖ **MAKE INFERENCES**

Look at Reading One again. Answer the question. Check (✓) all the correct answers. Then discuss your ideas with a partner.

Why do teenagers become Urban Angels?

Teenagers become Urban Angels to _____.

_✓_ **1.** become a member of a group

_✓_ **2.** meet friends

____ **3.** learn how to paint

____ **4.** get a nickname

____ **5.** find a job

____ **6.** leave the South Bronx

_✓_ **7.** avoid crime

____ **8.** make their parents happy

_✓_ **9.** help the South Bronx

____ **10.** your idea: _____

Hw

Write your answer to the question. Then share your answer with a partner or the class.

Do you think your neighborhood or city needs a program like Urban Angels? Explain your answer.

I (think / don't think) my neighborhood (or city) needs a program like Urban

Angels because _____.

B READING TWO: Two Real Angels

1 *Read about Kathy and Melissa.*

Two Real Angels

Kathy Santiago and Melissa Carrero are Urban Angels. Today they became Junior Associates—leaders of the younger Urban Angels.

"I don't smoke or take drugs. Those things are bad for me. Urban Angels teaches me to respect myself. I want to stay in school so I can become a fashion designer. I am confident that I can do it. I like Urban Angels because I like helping and teaching others. When I am older, I want to live in this neighborhood and continue to make life better for the people who live here."

—Kathy "Classy" Santiago, age 15

Urban Angels Kathy Santiago and Melissa Carrero

"At Urban Angels I learned that I can do anything. I want to be an actress. I can't do that if I join a gang. I am going to work and study hard. Plus, I have a little sister, and I know she watches me. I want to be a good example for her. We walk to school together in the morning. After school, I help her with her homework. We both get good grades. We know school is important. Hopefully, she will join Urban Angels, too."

—Melissa "Crazy Legs" Carrero, age 15

2 *Circle the correct answer to complete each sentence.*

1. The Urban Angels help Kathy and Melissa to ____.
   a. get a job
   b. be confident

2. In the future, Melissa wants to be ____.
   a. a fashion designer
   b. an actress

3. Both Kathy and Melissa ____.
   a. like teaching people
   b. want to be Guardian Angels

C INTEGRATE READINGS ONE AND TWO

◀ **STEP 1: Organize**

Look at Readings One and Two again. Fill in the chart with examples from Reading Two. Use the ideas in the list.

~~doesn't smoke or take drugs~~

gets good grades

teaches her sister about drugs and crime, helps her with her homework

wants to live in the neighborhood when she is an adult

wants to stay in school to become a fashion designer

won't join a gang

URBAN ANGELS TEACHES AT-RISK TEENAGERS TO . . .	KATHY . . .	MELISSA . . .
avoid drugs, gangs, guns, and crime	doesn't smoke or take drugs	
stay in school	wants to live in-- ~~	gets good grads
be positive members of the community / be role models	wants to stay. --	teaches her sister.-- won't join a gang

Look at Readings One and Two again. Then imagine that you are Melissa or Kathy. Write a letter to a friend. Tell your friend about your experience as an Urban Angel.

Nov. 20th, 2014

(Today's date)

Dear ___leon___,

(Your friend's name)

role model

Hi. How are you doing? I'm fine, but I miss you.

This year I joined the Urban Angels. I'm really excited about it. After school and on weekends, Urban Angels ___have educational and fun activites___

___ For example, we ___visit museams and clean up graffiti.___

I like being an Urban Angel because ___I want to help other teens___ I am learning to ___become an aspicial urban Angel member.___

If you move back to New York, I hope you will join the Urban Angels, too. I hope you are having fun in school this year. Write back soon.

Best regards,

Omran

(Your name)

H.w write a P. about an angel in your life

paragraph

③ FOCUS ON WRITING

Ⓐ VOCABULARY

◀ REVIEW

Complete the paragraphs with the words from the box. Use each word only once.

at-risk	crime	join	positive	role models	teenagers
avoid	grades	members	respect	support	~~urban~~

DISCIPLINE, ACTION, RESPONSIBILITY IN EDUCATION

DAREarts is a special program. The name stands for Discipline, Action, and Responsibility in Education. It is a program for kids in _____urban_____ areas. These kids are 9 to 14 years
1.
old. DAREarts is not just for _____teenagers_____.
2.

Kids in the DAREarts program study music, dance, theater, fashion, literature, and art history. DAREarts wants _____at-risk_____ kids to learn about the arts. They also want kids to _____avoid_____
3. **4.**
drugs, gangs, and _____crime_____. Kids also _____join_____ DAREarts to have fun. It is
5. **6.**
not like school—they do not get _____grades_____ like A, B+, or C.
7.

The DAREarts teachers (called "mentors") are famous artists. These artists are _____role models_____ for the DAREarts students. DAREarts students work with their teachers.
8.
Then they return to their schools and teach their classmates about art.

DAREarts helps young people feel good about themselves. They learn to _____respect_____ themselves because of their work. These kids become active
9.
_____members_____ of their school community. As a result, they do better in school, and they
10.
learn to see their future in a more _____positive_____ way.
11.
For information about how you can _____support_____ DAREarts, visit us at
12.
www.darearts.com.

◖ EXPAND

1 *Study the idioms.*

> **reach out to (someone):** *offer someone help*
>
> **give / lend (someone) a hand:** *help*
>
> **set a good / bad example:** *act in a way that other people might follow*
>
> 4 **fall through the cracks:** *not receive needed attention*

2 **Complete the conversations. Then practice them aloud with a partner.**

Conversation 1

ANDRE: Why do you work with at-risk teens? → *fall through the cracks*

BOB: If at-risk teens ~~I give a hand~~, they will have bigger problems as adults. They need our help today.

ANDRE: Yeah. You're right.

Conversation 2

PAMELA: Honey, I think you need to quit smoking.

RICHARD: I know, I know. But smoking helps me to relax.

PAMELA: But think of the kids! You don't want them to start smoking, do you? Don't *bad example*.

RICHARD: You're right, I'll try again to quit.

Conversation 3

HELEN: Can you *lend me hand* with this math problem?

MAX: Me? Sorry. I'm not a "math person." Ask Paula. She helps me with math all the time.

Conversation 4

TOM: My father always tells me to *reach out to* people who need help. Don't wait for them to ask you for help.

MICHAEL: Yeah. Sometimes we all need a helping hand.

❰ CREATE

Imagine that you have a friend in another town. Your friend is writing a report about teenagers. Complete the letter. Tell your friend about teenagers in your town. Use some of the words from Review and Expand.

_____
(Date)

Dear ___ *salm* ___,
(Name of friend or family member)

In sociology class, we are learning about at-risk teens in urban areas. Let me tell you about teenagers in my community.

Most teens here do not have problems. They _____

_____

But some teens have problems, such as _____

_____ They _____

_____

_____

I _____

_____

I hope _____

_____

Let me know if you need more information.

_____
(Your name)

1 *Read the paragraph. Look at the underlined words. Draw an arrow from each underlined word to the noun it refers to. Then answer the questions.*

What Do Urban Angels Do?

Urban Angels have many activities after school and on Saturdays. They go on trips to local museums and to other places outside the city. They also visit businesses to learn about different jobs. Most important, Urban Angels help out in their community. At "park clean-ups" they go to city parks and make them beautiful again.

1. Which underlined word is a subject?
2. Which underlined word is an object?
3. Which underlined word shows possession?

PRONOUNS AND POSSESSIVE ADJECTIVES

A **pronoun** is a word that takes the place of a noun. Pronouns are useful when you don't want to repeat a noun in a sentence.	[subject] **Urban Angels** have many activities.
I. Subject pronouns take the place of the subject in a sentence. Subject pronouns include: *I, you, he, she, it, we,* and *they*.	[subject / pronoun] **They** go on trips to local museums. **You** can become an Urban Angel.
2. Object pronouns take the place of an object. Objects usually come after the verb. Object pronouns also come after prepositions like *for, to,* and *from*. Object pronouns include: *me, you, him, her, it, us,* and *them*.	[object] Urban Angels like to help **people**. [object pronoun] Urban Angels teach **them** about safety. The Urban Angels program needs **support**. New York City helps pay for **it**.
3. Possessive adjectives are like pronouns. They show possession or ownership. They always come before a noun. Possessive adjectives include: *my, your, his, her, its, our,* and *their*.	Urban Angels help out in **their** community. **My** goal is to be a fashion designer. Kelly isn't an Urban Angel, but **her** friend is.

2 *Read the sentences about Curtis Sliwa. Complete each sentence with **he**, **him**, or **his**.*

1. Curtis Sliwa started a recycling program when _____he_____ was only 14 years old.

2. _____He_____ used the money from recycling to help children in _____his_____ neighborhood.

3. When _____he_____ was 15 years old, _____he_____ saved a family from a fire in their house.

4. The *New York Daily News* named _____him_____ "Boy of the Year."

5. When _____he_____ was 16 years old, _____he_____ went to the White House.

6. President Nixon gave _____him_____ an award for _____his_____ community service.

7. After high school, _____he_____ worked at a McDonald's restaurant in the South Bronx.

8. _____He_____ started a community clean-up program.

9. Other McDonald's employees helped _____him_____ .

10. _____He_____ started the Guardian Angels in 1979.

11. When _____he_____ was young, _____his_____ parents taught _____him_____ to take care of the community.

12. _____He_____ is still taking care of his community today.

3 *Wanda "Lipstick" Ayala is a Guardian Angel. Read the paragraphs about Wanda. Complete the sentences with* **she**, **her**, **he**, **they**, *or* **them**.

Wanda "Lipstick" Ayala

Wanda "Lipstick" Ayala is 35 years old. __She__ lives in
1.
Washington, D.C., with __her__
2.
three children and __her__
3.
husband. __she__ works for the
4.
United States Postal Service.

__she__ also helps out in
5.
__her__ community.
6.

Lipstick and __her__ little
7.
brother grew up in a dangerous neighborhood in Washington, D.C.

__they__ loved each other very much. For many years, Wanda tried to
8.
protect __her__ brother from drugs. Unfortunately, __he__ had a drug
9.   10.
problem, and __he__ died in 1996.
11.

After __her__ brother died, Lipstick became a Guardian Angel.
12.
__Her__ nickname is "Lipstick" because __she__ always wears bright red
13.   14.
lipstick. In __her__ free time, __she__ helps young children and
15.   16.
teenagers. Wanda says, "All children are important. People have to take care
of __them__."
17.

In this unit, you read about the Urban Angels.

You are going to **write a letter to the editor of a local newspaper telling why you support a group that helps your community**. Tell who you are and why you support the group. Use the vocabulary and grammar from the unit.*

◀ **PREPARE TO WRITE: Making a List**

To help you organize your ideas for your letter, you are going to **make a list** as a prewriting activity. When you make a list, do not write complete sentences.

1 *Work with the class. Make a list of organizations that help your community. Think of organizations that help children or teenagers, teach about art, music, drama, science, sports, or a hobby, or support animals, health, social issues, or religion. Write them in the chart.*

ORGANIZATIONS	WHO OR WHAT DO THEY HELP?	WHAT DO THEY DO? GIVE EXAMPLES.
Urban Angels	yung people, How are at-risk	They help teenages to avoid drugs
DAREarts	～	～
Al Kashava	People who need help	colleting the blood for public hospitls
Al Helal Al Ahmer	～ ～	Help old People. who need help. (seniors)

*For Alternative Writing Topics, see page 105. These topics can be used in place of the writing topic for this unit or as homework. The alternative topics relate to the theme of the unit, but may not target the same grammar or rhetorical structures taught in the unit.

2 *Choose one organization to write about on a separate piece of paper. Make a list of all the ways the organization helps your community.*

Example

Urban Angels

- help teens stay in school
- help teens avoid drugs, gangs, guns, crime
- go to museums
- visit businesses
- have after-school and weekend activities
- take classes and learn about social issues
- learn to be role models

◖ WRITE: A Letter to the Editor

People write letters to the editor of a newspaper to share their opinions with the community. Letters to the editor are in the newspaper for everyone to read.

A letter to the editor tells:
- who you are (a student, a teacher, or a police officer)
- which community organization you are writing about
- why you support the organization

1 *Read the letter to the editor. Then read the questions and the answers.*

March 18, 2009

Dear Editor,

I am a student in New York City. I am writing about a program called the Urban Angels. Urban Angels help teens avoid problems such as drugs, crime, and gangs. They want teens to stay in school. Urban Angels have activities after school and on weekends. In addition, Urban Angels help the community. Teens can take classes about social issues. They learn how to take care of themselves and stop problems in the community. Finally, Urban Angels help their city. For example, they paint over graffiti at neighborhood "paint-outs." At "park clean-ups," they go to city parks and make them beautiful again. For all these reasons, I think people should support the Urban Angels program.

Sincerely,

Maurice Roberts

Maurice Roberts

1. Who is Maurice Roberts?

   A student from New York City.

2. Which group is he writing about?

   He's writing about the Urban Angels.

3. Why does he support this group?

   He supports the Urban Angels because they help teens avoid

   problems and stay in school. They also help their community and

   their city.

2 *Read the letter to the editor. Then answer the questions.*

September 10, 2009

Dear Editor,

I am a high school art teacher. I am writing about the Neighborhood Arts Center (NAC). The NAC has art classes for children and adults. Children can take classes after school. There are classes for adults in the evenings and on weekends. The NAC also supports local artists. Local artists teach the classes at the NAC. The NAC gift shop sells paintings and other art by local artists. For all these reasons, I think people should support the NAC.

Sincerely,

Maude Moran

Maude Moran

1. Who is Maude Moran?

   She's a highschool art teacher.

2. Which community organization is she writing about?

   She's writing about the Neighborhood Art center.

3. Why does she support the organization?

   The NAC has art classes for children. and in addition NAC supports local artists

3 *Think about the organization you chose in Prepare to Write, Exercise 2, on page 100. Read your list of ways the organization helps your community. Choose two or three ways to include in your letter.*

4 *Write your first draft. Include a topic sentence that gives the main idea of your paragraph. Write sentences to explain or support the main idea. Don't worry about grammar yet. Just try to make your ideas clear.*

Examples are pieces of information that support an opinion. There are several ways to introduce examples:

Use *such as* to introduce examples in a sentence. A list of things often follows *such as*.

> The Urban Angels help teens avoid problems such as drugs, crimes, and gangs.

Use *for example* to introduce an example in a new sentence. A comma and a complete sentence follow *for example*.

> The Urban Angels help the city. For example, they paint over graffiti at neighborhood "paint-outs."

1 *Look back at the letter in Write, Exercise 1, on page 101. Underline the sentences with **such as** and **for example**.*

2 *Read the statements and examples about the Neighborhood Arts Center on pages 103 and 104. Rewrite each statement and example in one or two complete sentences. Introduce each example with **such as** or **for example**.*

    1. *Statement:*   The Neighborhood Arts Center helps children.

      Example(s):   Children can learn about art.

      Complete sentence(s):   The Neighborhood Arts Center helps children. For example, children can learn about art.

    2. *Statement:*   The Neighborhood Arts Center has many arts classes.

      Example(s):   painting, drawing, and sculpture

      Complete sentence(s):   The Neighborhood Arts Center has many art classes such as painting, drawing, and sculpture.

(continued on next page)

3. *Statement:* The Neighborhood Arts Center has classes for all ages.

   Example(s): children, college students, adults, and senior citizens

   Complete sentence(s): The NAC has classes for all ages such as children, college students, adults, and senior citizens

4. *Statement:* The art classes are not expensive.

   Example(s): A drawing class costs $15 per semester.

   Completes sentence(s): The art classes are not expensive, for example, a drawing class costs $15 per semester

5. *Statement:* The Neighborhood Arts Center supports local artists.

   Example(s): Local artists teach classes at the Arts Center.

   Complete sentence(s): The Neighborhood Arts Center supports local artists, for example, local artists teach ---

6. *Statement:* The gift shop sells art by local artists.

   Example(s): jewelry, paintings, and pottery

   Complete sentence(s): The gift shop sells art by - --- such as jewelry, pi --- -

for example, such as, in additional, furthermore

finally

◀ **EDIT: Writing the Final Draft**

Prepare to write the final draft of your letter. Check your grammar, spelling, capitalization, and punctuation. Check that you used some of the vocabulary and grammar from the unit. Use the checklist to help you write your final draft. Then neatly write or type your letter.

✓ FINAL DRAFT CHECKLIST

○ Did you write about an organization that helps your community?
○ Did you say who you are?
○ Did you include examples to support your opinion?
○ Did you use *such as* and *for example* to introduce your examples?
○ Did you use pronouns and possessive adjectives correctly?
○ Did you format the letter correctly?
○ Did you use vocabulary from the unit?

ALTERNATIVE WRITING TOPICS

Write about one of the topics. Use the vocabulary and grammar from the unit.

1. What is one way people are trying to help at-risk young people in your school or community? Write a paragraph. First describe the problem. Then write about how people are trying to help at-risk young people.

2. Guardian Angels and Urban Angels have nicknames. Their nicknames say something about their personalities and their goals.

   Do you have a nickname now? Did you have one in the past? What is it? Do you like it? How did you get this nickname?

   If you don't have a nickname, choose one for yourself. Then explain how this nickname fits your personality and your goals for the future. Write a paragraph about your nickname.

RESEARCH TOPICS, see page 220.

UNIT 6

Going Out of Business?

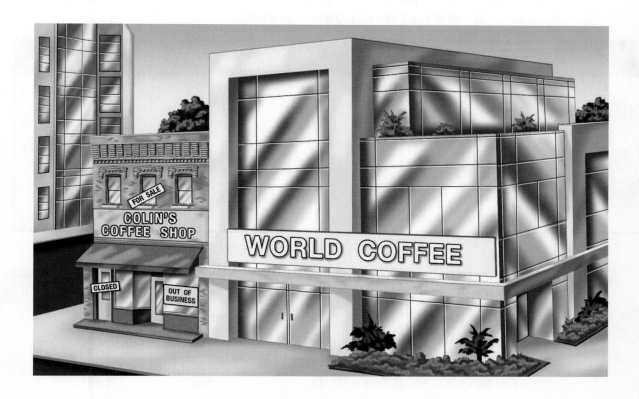

1 FOCUS ON THE TOPIC

A PREDICT

Look at the picture. Discuss the questions with the class.

1. Is Colin's Coffee Shop open or closed? How do you know?

2. What does *out of business* mean?

3. Is there a store in your city or community that went out of business? Explain.

107

Chain stores are usually owned by large companies. A chain has many stores with the same name. You will read about actual chain stores. For example, Starbucks® is a chain of coffee bars. *Locally-owned businesses* (also called *family-owned businesses*) are usually small and owned by people in the community.

1 *Work in a small group. Make a list of the stores in your city or community. Put them in two groups: **locally owned** or **chain**.*

LOCALLY OWNED	CHAIN

2 *Do you go to the stores on your lists? Talk with your group about why or why not. Use the possible reasons below or think of your own reasons.*

Positive Reasons

It has more products.
I like the products.
The service is good.
It is near my home.

Negative Reasons

It doesn't have the things I want.
I don't like the products.
The service isn't good.
It's too far away from my home.

Your own reasons: _____

_____

_____

_____

1 *Match the phrases on the left with the places on the right.*

_____ 1. buy books or magazines

_____ 2. buy materials and tools to build or fix
things in your home

_____ 3. get some medicine

_____ 4. rent a movie

_____ 5. buy pens, pencils, or paper

_____ 6. buy a TV, DVD player, or computer

_____ 7. get a haircut

a. electronics store

b. video store

c. barbershop

d. bookstore

e. hardware store

f. office supply store

g. drugstore

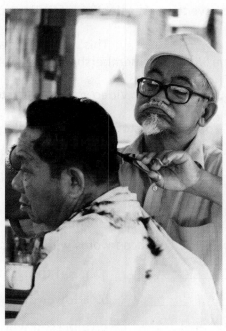

2 *Write sentences using the words and phrases in Exercise 1.*

1. _I can buy books or magazines at a bookstore._____

2. _____

3. _____

4. _____

5. _____

6. _____

7. _____

3 *Read the ad for Captain Video®.*

 **CAPTAIN VIDEO**

1034 High Ridge Road   Stamford, CT 04586
1–878–CAPTAIN

Get your favorite DVDs and video games.
Be a Captain Video member today!

The **benefits** of being a member are:

▶ Lowest prices: Other video stores can't **compete** with our low prices.

▶ Great service: Our **employees** will help you find the DVDs and video games you want.

▶ Selection: We have the best **selection** of DVDs and video games—more than 15,000!

This week's special:
Get a $50 family membership for only $45! That's a $5 **discount**!

At Captain Video you—our **customers**—are #1.

Thanks to you—our **loyal** customers—for shopping at Captain Video for over 20 years!

Richard Woodroof,
Owner of Captain Video

4 *Match the boldfaced words with their definitions. Write the word on the line.*

_____ **a.** good things; things that are helpful to you

_____ **b.** a lower price than usual

_____ **c.** a person who has or owns something

_____ **d.** not changing; faithful

_____ **e.** people who buy things from a store or company

_____ **f.** to try to be the best at something

_____ **g.** people who work in a store or for a company

_____ **h.** choice

2 FOCUS ON READING

A READING ONE: The Death of the Family-Owned Video Store?

Richard Woodroof is the owner of Captain Video. Captain Video is a family-owned video store in Stamford, Connecticut. Mr. Woodroof sends a newsletter to all his customers. The newsletter is called *The Captain's Call*.

1 *Work with a partner. Before you read, think about* The Captain's Call. *Check (✓) the words you think you will see in this newsletter.*

_____ community	_____ goal	_____ service
_____ expert	_____ online	_____ support
_____ gallery	_____ rare	_____ volunteer

2 *Read the article from* The Captain's Call.

THE CAPTAIN'S CALL

Summer Edition Volume 2.2   *1034 High Ridge Road Stamford, CT*

The Death of the Family-Owned Video Store?

1 Large chain stores are killing family-owned businesses in Stamford. First, Borders Books®, a large chain store, opened, and then a small **bookstore** went out of business. Then Rite Aid®, a large **drugstore** chain, opened, and a small drugstore went out of business. Small stores can't **compete** with these large chain stores.

2 Other family-owned businesses in Stamford are in danger: a **hardware store**, a **barbershop**, an **office supply store**, an **electronics store**, and a **video store**—Captain Video! If you don't do something now, your life in Stamford will change forever.

3 Today, a big video chain store, Blockbuster®, opened in Stamford. Now, our store is in danger.

4 Captain Video can stay in business only if you help. You, our **loyal customers**, know the **benefits** Captain Video offers. They are:

5 ▶ Selection—We have more movies than other video stores in Stamford. We have more than 15,000 DVDs and video games. We are always adding more.

6 ▶ Service—The **employees** at Captain Video love movies and know a lot about them, so we can give personal service to all our customers.

7 ▶ Prices—Because of competition with Blockbuster, we had to increase our prices a little. But we still have great **discounts**. For example, when you rent more than one movie, you pay less. We also have longer rental times on most DVDs and games.

8 Thank you for being loyal customers. Please continue to support Captain Video and other family-owned businesses. With your support, we can stay open.

9 Life in Stamford will change forever without family-owned businesses. Only YOU can stop the chain stores from changing Stamford!

◖ READ FOR MAIN IDEAS

Read each pair of sentences. Check (✓) the sentence that is true.

1. _____ **a.** Blockbuster is in danger of going out of business.

    _✓_ **b.** Captain Video is in danger of going out of business.

2. _____ **a.** Small, locally-owned stores are closing in Stamford.

    _____ **b.** Large chain stores are closing in Stamford.

3. _____ **a.** Mr. Woodroof wants the customers to support the chain stores.

    _____ **b.** Mr. Woodroof wants the customers to support the smaller stores.

4. _____ **a.** Mr. Woodroof is afraid that life in his town is changing.

    _____ **b.** Mr. Woodroof is happy that life in his town is changing.

◖ READ FOR DETAILS

Read each sentence. Circle the correct answer to complete each sentence.

1. Borders is the name of a large _____ chain.

    a. (bookstore)   **c.** electronics store

    b. drugstore   **d.** video store

2. Captain Video is trying to compete with _____.

    a. video stores   **c.** drugstores

    b. bookstores   **d.** coffee bars

3. Captain Video has more _____ than other video stores in Stamford.

    a. customers   **c.** movies

    b. employees   **d.** video games

4. Captain Video's customers are _____.

    a. changing   **c.** loyal

    b. friendly   **d.** personal

(continued on next page)

5. Captain Video's employees know a lot about _____.

   a. chain stores   **c.** video games

   b. customers   **d.** movies

6. Captain Video recently increased its _____.

   a. prices   **c.** employees

   b. videos   **d.** customers

7. Captain Video has special _____ on video rentals.

   a. selections   **c.** customers

   b. discounts   **d.** service

◖ MAKE INFERENCES

Work with a partner. Read each sentence. Why is Richard Woodroof upset?
*Write **T** (true) or **F** (false). Then discuss your answers with the class.*

_____ **1.** He doesn't want life in Stamford to change.

_____ **2.** He doesn't want his personal life to change.

_____ **3.** He doesn't like competition.

_____ **4.** He might lose his business.

_____ **5.** He is worried about his customers.

_____ **6.** He thinks all chain stores are bad.

◖ EXPRESS OPINIONS

Read the question. Check (✓) your answer and write a reason. Then compare
your answers with a partner's.

Will Captain Video stay open?

_____ Yes, Captain Video will stay open because _____

_____

_____ No, Captain Video will not stay open because _____

_____

1 *Read the information about Blockbuster's online service.*

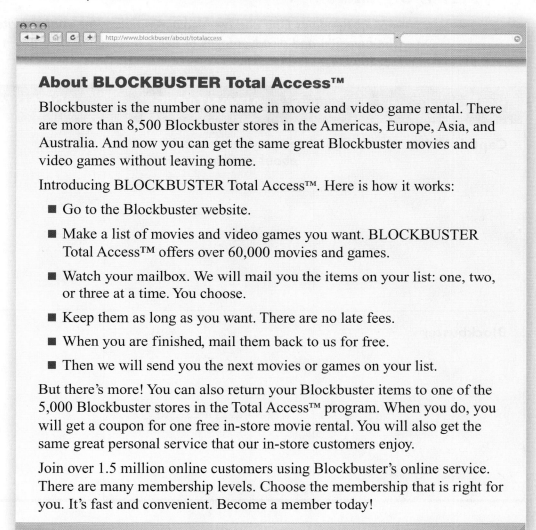

> ### About BLOCKBUSTER Total Access™
>
> Blockbuster is the number one name in movie and video game rental. There are more than 8,500 Blockbuster stores in the Americas, Europe, Asia, and Australia. And now you can get the same great Blockbuster movies and video games without leaving home.
>
> Introducing BLOCKBUSTER Total Access™. Here is how it works:
>
> - Go to the Blockbuster website.
> - Make a list of movies and video games you want. BLOCKBUSTER Total Access™ offers over 60,000 movies and games.
> - Watch your mailbox. We will mail you the items on your list: one, two, or three at a time. You choose.
> - Keep them as long as you want. There are no late fees.
> - When you are finished, mail them back to us for free.
> - Then we will send you the next movies or games on your list.
>
> But there's more! You can also return your Blockbuster items to one of the 5,000 Blockbuster stores in the Total Access™ program. When you do, you will get a coupon for one free in-store movie rental. You will also get the same great personal service that our in-store customers enjoy.
>
> Join over 1.5 million online customers using Blockbuster's online service. There are many membership levels. Choose the membership that is right for you. It's fast and convenient. Become a member today!

2 *Complete the sentences with the correct numbers.*

1. There are more than _____ Blockbuster stores.

2. There are _____ stores in the BLOCKBUSTER Total Access program.

3. You can choose from more than _____ movies and games online.

4. Blockbuster has _____ million online customers.

◀ **STEP 1: Organize**

Look at Readings One and Two again. Complete the chart. Write the advantages (the benefits) and disadvantages of being a customer at Captain Video and Blockbuster.

	ADVANTAGES	DISADVANTAGES
Captain Video	employees know a lot about movies	
Blockbuster		

◀ **STEP 2: Synthesize**

Complete the conversation between Mr. Woodroof and a Captain Video customer who now uses Blockbuster. Talk about the advantages and disadvantages from Organize.

CUSTOMER: Hi, Richard.

WOODROOF: Hello, Larry. Long time no see!

CUSTOMER: Yeah. Sorry about that. I'm not a member of Captain Video

anymore.

WOODROOF: But why not? Captain Video _____

(Talk about two advantages of Captain Video.)

_____

_____

CUSTOMER: I know, Richard, but _____

(Talk about the disadvantages of Captain Video.)

_____

_____

Blockbuster Total Access _____

_____

(Talk about the advantages of Blockbuster Total Access.)

_____

WOODROOF: Well, maybe Captain Video will offer the same services as

BLOCKBUSTER Total Access.

CUSTOMER: That would be great.

③ FOCUS ON WRITING

Ⓐ VOCABULARY

◖ REVIEW

Read the review of the movie You've Got Mail *on the next page. Fill in the blanks with the words from the box. Use each word only once.*

benefit	coupons	employees	owner
~~bookstore~~	customers	enjoyed	selection
compete	discounts	loyal	

Movie Review

You've Got Mail is a romantic comedy about two __bookstore__ owners, Kathleen and Joe. They meet in a chat room. As they e-mail each other, they start to fall in love.

Kathleen Kelly (actress Meg Ryan) is the _____ of a children's bookstore. Her mother started this small bookstore when Kelly was a little girl. Kelly offers her _____ a lot of personal service. Personal service is the biggest _____ of shopping at Kelly's store. She can't offer her customers _____ for books because her company needs the money.

Joe Fox (actor Tom Hanks) is the owner of Fox Books, a large bookstore chain in New York. Fox Books has a large _____ of books. It also offers big _____ on its books.

Some of Kelly's _____ customers start to shop at Fox Books. But Fox's _____ do not know a lot about children's books. Kelly knows a lot about children's books. She always _____ reading books to her young customers.

Can Kelly's family-owned bookstore _____ with the big chain store? Will Fox and Kelly live happily ever after? Watch *You've Got Mail* and find out.

Look at the chart. It shows some important word forms. (It does not give all the possible word forms.) Then complete the sentences.

NOUN	ADJECTIVE	VERB
benefit	beneficial	benefit
competition, competitor	competitive	compete
employee	employed	employ
loyalty	loyal	***
service	***	serve
owner	***	own

1. **(compete / competition / competitive / competitors)**

   McDonald's® and Burger King® are _____. They are both fast-food restaurants.

   McDonald's and Burger King _____ for more customers.

   The _____ between McDonald's and Burger King's is very strong.

   The owners of these two companies are very _____ people. They like to win.

2. **(employed / employees / employs)**

   Starbucks _____ over 79,000 people around the word.

   At Starbucks, _____ are called "partners."

   I am not _____ right now. Maybe I can get a job at Starbucks.

3. **(benefits / benefited / beneficial)**

   There are many _____ for Starbucks employees.

   Last year our community _____ from Starbucks. This year the same will happen.

   Some people think chain stores are not _____ to communities.

   (continued on next page)

4. **(loyal / loyalty)**

Our _____ customers always come to our store.

We need your _____ to stay in business.

5. **(own / owner / owns)**

Colin, my brother, _____ three coffee shops.

Colin is the _____ of three coffee shops.

My brother and sister _____ one coffee shop together.

6. **(serve / serves / service)**

Colin's Coffee Shop _____ a lot of coffee every day.

The employees at Colin's _____ their customers with a smile.

The _____ at Colin's is usually fast.

(CREATE

Write a paragraph about a store, restaurant, or business you know. Why do you go there? (Or, why don't you go there?) Think about locally-owned stores or chain stories. Use some of the vocabulary from Review and Expand.

_____

_____

_____

_____

_____

_____

_____

_____

_____

Young-Hee and Sofia are friends. Young-Hee is from Korea, and Sofia is from Australia. They spent four years at the same university in the United States. Young-Hee returned home to Korea, and Sofia went back to Australia. Then Young-Hee wrote Sofia an e-mail.

1 *Read Young-Hee's e-mail. Then answer the questions. Discuss your answers with a partner.*

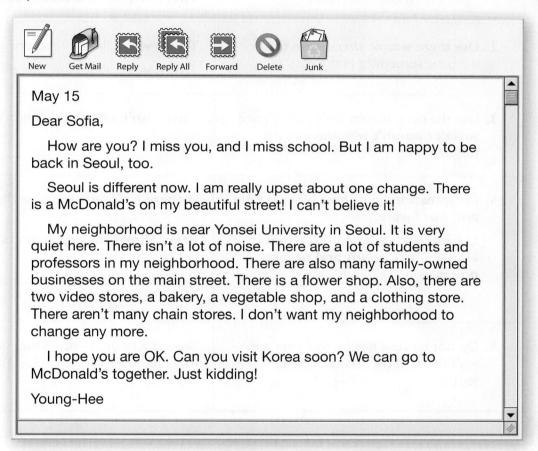

New   Get Mail   Reply   Reply All   Forward   Delete   Junk

May 15

Dear Sofia,

How are you? I miss you, and I miss school. But I am happy to be back in Seoul, too.

Seoul is different now. I am really upset about one change. There is a McDonald's on my beautiful street! I can't believe it!

My neighborhood is near Yonsei University in Seoul. It is very quiet here. There isn't a lot of noise. There are a lot of students and professors in my neighborhood. There are also many family-owned businesses on the main street. There is a flower shop. Also, there are two video stores, a bakery, a vegetable shop, and a clothing store. There aren't many chain stores. I don't want my neighborhood to change any more.

I hope you are OK. Can you visit Korea soon? We can go to McDonald's together. Just kidding!

Young-Hee

1. How many times does Young-Hee use *there is, there isn't, there are,* and *there aren't*? Underline them.

2. What nouns follow *there is* and *there isn't*? Make a list.

3. What nouns follow *there are* and *there aren't*? Make a list.

THERE IS / THERE ARE

1. Use **there is** or **there are** to describe something in the **present**.

   There is + singular count noun

   There are + plural count noun

   There is + non-count noun

   There is a bank on Main Street.

   There are a lot of students in my neighborhood.

   There is a lot of traffic in Seoul.

2. Use **there was** or **there were** to describe something in the past.

   There was a flower shop on my street.

   There were a lot of people on my street.

3. Use the contractions **isn't / aren't** and **wasn't / weren't** with **there** in the **negative**.

   There isn't a McDonald's nearby.

4. For **questions**, put **there** after **is / are** and **was / were**.

   Use **any** with **yes / no** questions **about plural nouns and non-count nouns**.

   Is there a movie theater nearby?

   Were there any restaurants in your neighborhood?

   Is there any traffic in your neighborhood at night?

5. Do not confuse *there is* and *there are* with *there*. *There* means "in that location."

   Seoul is a beautiful city. There are some beautiful parks **there** (in Seoul).

2 *Read Sofia's reply to Young-Hee. Then choose the correct verbs to complete her sentences.*

New   Get Mail   Reply   Reply All   Forward   Delete   Junk

June 25

Dear Young-Hee,

Thanks for your e-mail. I miss you, too. But I don't miss school!
There _____ a lot of changes here in Perth, too. I'm really
1. (is / are)
surprised!

My street is quiet, but there _____ two busy streets
2. (is / are)
nearby, Main Street and Queens Road. There _____ a lot
3. (is / are)
of cars on these streets. When I was young, there _____
4. (wasn't / weren't)
much noise, but today there _____ more people and cars.
5. (is / are)

Here's another change. There _____ two Starbucks
6. (is / are)
near my apartment! Two! Five years ago there _____ only
7. (was / were)
one small café. I ate breakfast there every morning. But it's gone!
There _____ a hardware store there now.
8. (is / are)

Luckily, one thing did not change. There _____ still a
9. (is / are)
beautiful old movie theater on the corner of Main Street and

Queens Road. It's called the Astor Theater. It is one of my favorite

places. _____ there any chance you can visit me in
10. (Is / Are)
Australia? I hope to visit you in Korea soon.

Sofia

3 Work with a partner. Write five questions to ask about your partner's neighborhood or city. Use **Is / Are there** and **Was / Were there**. Then exchange books and answer each other's questions. Use **There is / are** and **There was / were**.

1. a. <u>Are there any fast-food restaurants nearby?</u>

   b. <u>Yes, there is. There is a McDonald's.</u>

2. a. _____

   b. _____

3. a. _____

   b. _____

4. a. _____

   b. _____

5. a. _____

   b. _____

6. a. _____

   b. _____

C WRITING

In this unit, you read about family-owned businesses and chain stores.

You are going to **write a paragraph describing one of your favorite places, such as a store or a restaurant**. Use the vocabulary and grammar from the unit.*

PREPARE TO WRITE: Drawing a Map

To help you think of a place to describe, you will draw a map as a prewriting activity.

1 Work with a partner. Talk about the stores and restaurants you like. Here are some places. Write one example of each place.

---

*For Alternative Writing Topics, see page 129. These topics can be used in place of the writing topic for this unit or as homework. The alternative topics relate to the theme of the unit, but may not target the same grammar or rhetorical structures taught in the unit.

Places	Examples
Restaurant	<u>The Big Salad</u>
Department store	_____
Video store	_____
Clothing store	_____
Grocery (food) store	_____
Bookstore	_____
Other	_____

2 *Work with a partner. Look at the picture of The Big Salad. Answer the questions.*

    1. What kind of place is The Big Salad?

    2. Where is it? What is nearby?

3 *Look at your list from Exercise 1. Choose one place to write about. Draw a map of the store or restaurant on a separate piece of paper. Draw the things inside and the area around it.*

4 *Work with a partner. Look at your partner's map and ask your partner the questions. Then your partner will ask you the questions about your map.*

    1. What place is the writer describing?

    2. Where is it? What is nearby?

    3. What does it sell?

    4. What is the atmosphere (the feeling inside the place) like?

    5. Why do you like it?

◀ **WRITE: A Description of a Place**

When you write a **description** of a place, you use words that describe how things look, feel, smell, taste, or sound.

1 *Read the paragraph. Work with a partner. Answer the questions.*

> I like The Big Salad. The Big Salad is on Main Street. It is next to the post office and across from the department store. When you walk in the door, you smell fresh bread. There is a large salad bar. There are also tasty soups, such as chicken noodle, clam chowder, and onion. I also like the atmosphere. There are big windows in the front. It is very bright and cheerful. The Big Salad is a great place to eat.

1. What place is the writer describing?

2. Where is it? What is nearby?

3. What does it sell?

4. What is the atmosphere like?

5. Why does the writer like it?

2 *Read the paragraph again. Make a list of the descriptive words. The list is started for you.*

fresh	_____	_____	_____
large	_____	_____	

3 *Complete the paragraph on the next page with the descriptive words or phrases from the box.*

big	friendly	near my house
comfortable	~~interesting~~	next to the window

The Night Owl Bookshop is a great place to buy books. It is open late

at night. It has a lot of _____interesting_____ books. For example, it has a

1.

_____ selection of comic books. I also like the atmosphere in

2.

The Night Owl. There are a lot of _____ chairs. My favorite

3.

chair is _____. The employees are very _____.

4.   5.

They always say hello. I'm glad that The Night Owl Bookshop is

_____.

6.

4 *Now you are ready to write you first draft. Don't worry about the grammar.*
Just try to make your ideas clear.

◖**REVISE: Describing a Place Using Space Order**

Space order means organizing ideas by location or place. For example, you
can go from left to right, up or down, or around or across.

DESCRIBING A PLACE USING SPACE ORDER

Use prepositions to show location:

across (from)	in front of	on the right
around the corner (from)	next to	to the left (of)
behind	on	to the right (of)
between	on the left	

When you describe a place with space order, your reader will understand you more easily.

---

1 *Read the paragraph about High Ridge Road in Stamford, Connecticut. As you read, continue drawing the arrow (→) from place to place. Then compare your arrows with your classmates'.*

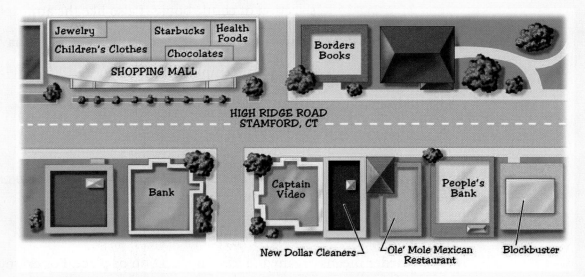

Captain Video is on High Ridge Road in Stamford, CT. There are a lot of businesses near Captain Video. Across the street from Captain Video is a bank. Across High Ridge Road from the bank is a shopping mall. On the left is a children's clothing store. Behind that store is a jewelry store. To the right of the children's clothing store are a Starbucks, a health food store, and a chocolate shop. Next to the mall and directly across from Captain Video is Borders Books. New Dollar Cleaners is next to Captain Video. Olé Mole Mexican restaurant is next to the cleaners. People's Bank is next to that. Just four doors away from Captain Video is Blockbuster.

2 *Look back at the map in Prepare to Write, Exercise 2, on page 125. Complete the sentences. Circle the correct preposition.*

1. The Big Salad is (*at* / *on*) Main Street.

2. The Big Salad is (*across from* / *next to*) the bank.

3. It is (*between* / *around the corner from*) the post office and the department store.

4. The front door of The Big Salad is (*behind* / *around the corner from*) the post office.

5. The Big Salad is (*behind* / *across from*) the department store.

6. There are tables (*between* / *in front of*) the big windows.

7. The salad bar is (*around the corner from* / *to the right of*) the cashier.

3 Look at the first draft of your paragraph. Do you use space descriptions to describe location? If not, add one or two space descriptions to your paragraph. Describe the location of the store or restaurant and what it looks like inside.

◀ **EDIT: Writing the Final Draft**

Prepare to write the final draft of your paragraph. Check your grammar, spelling, capitalization, and punctuation. Check that you used some of the vocabulary and grammar from the unit. Use the checklist to help you write your final draft. Then neatly write or type your paragraph.

✔ FINAL DRAFT CHECKLIST

- ○ Did you describe a place?
- ○ Did you use *there is* and *there are* correctly?
- ○ Did you use space description?
- ○ Did you use vocabulary from the unit?

ALTERNATIVE WRITING TOPICS

Write about one of the topics. Use the vocabulary and grammar from the unit.

1. Write about your neighborhood or city. Are there any changes? Do things look different from five or ten years ago? Write a short paragraph. Use space order.

2. Is your city or town a good place to live? Is it a good place for businesses? Explain your answer in two paragraphs. Write one paragraph for each question.

3. In many places, large businesses are becoming more popular. Small, family-owned businesses are going out of business. Is this a good change? Write your answer in one paragraph.

RESEARCH TOPICS, see page 221.

UNIT 7

Flying High and Low

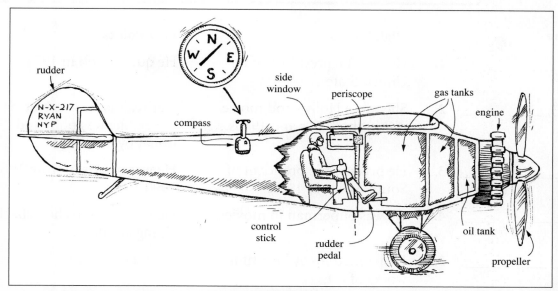

Spirit of St. Louis

①FOCUS ON THE TOPIC

A PREDICT

Look at the picture. Discuss the questions with the class.

1. What is the *Spirit of St. Louis*?

2. How old do you think the *Spirit of St. Louis* is? Explain.

3. Do you want to take a long trip in this airplane? Why or why not?

131

1 *Famous people have high points (good times) and low points (bad times) in their lives. Work with a partner. Look at the list of names. Write the correct name next to the high point and low point in that person's life. Compare your answers with others' in the class.*

Nelson Mandela	Richard Nixon	Diana Spencer	Pu Yi
Marilyn Monroe	Christopher Reeve	Vincent van Gogh	

Name		High Points	Low Points
_____	1.	He was the president of the United States.	He quit his job in 1974.
_____	2.	She was a Hollywood movie star in the 1950s and 1960s.	Her real name was Norma Jean Baker. She was poor and unhappy as a child.
_____	3.	He became the president of South Africa in 1994.	He was in prison from 1964 to 1990.
_____	4.	He was Superman in movies.	He had a serious horseback riding accident.
_____	5.	He painted many beautiful works of art.	He cut off his ear.
_____	6.	He was the emperor of China.	He lost his empire.
_____	7.	She was a teacher and became a princess.	Her marriage to Prince Charles ended.

2 *Work with a partner. Interview each other. Ask: What was a high point in your life? What was a low point? Then answer your partner's questions.*

Read the words and their definitions. Then read about Lindbergh's trip on the Spirit of St. Louis. Complete the sentences with words from the list.

pilot: the person who flies an airplane

flight: a trip in an airplane

took off: left a place in an airplane (past form of *take off*)

landed: arrived somewhere in an airplane

set a record: to do something faster or better than ever before

media: (*plural*) newspapers, magazines, radio, and television

contest: a game that people try to win; a competition

~~**handsome:** good-looking (usually for a man)~~

hero: someone you respect very much for doing something good

In 1919, Raymond Orteig started a competition. He offered $25,000 to the first pilot to fly non-stop across the Atlantic Ocean between New York and Paris. In 1927, Charles Lindbergh was the winner.

In the 1920s flying airplanes was a new science. Charles Lindbergh, a _____handsome_____ young airmail _____, was very interested in
       1.   2.

flying. On May 10, 1927, Lindbergh _____ from San Diego,
                                3.

California. He stopped in St. Louis, Missouri, for gas and oil. Then he quickly continued on to New York to enter Raymond Orteig's _____.
                                                   4.

He _____ in New York on May 12th. He flew from San
      5.

Diego to New York in less than 22 hours. He _____ for the
                                        6.

fastest _____ across the United States.
           7.

This was only the beginning of Lindbergh's historic trip. Lindbergh was on his way to becoming an international _____. The
                                            8.

_____ followed him from that time on.
   9.

② FOCUS ON READING

A READING ONE: Lindbergh Did It!

RAYMOND ORTEIG PRESENTS
Win $25,000

IRELAND

ST. LOUIS • NEW YORK CITY
SAN DIEGO

PARIS

Be the first person to fly non-stop across the ATLANTIC OCEAN!

1 *A **fool** is a person who is crazy or not very intelligent. At first, people called Lindbergh "The Flying Fool." Why do you think they called him this? Check (✓) the answers you think are correct.*

_____ The weather was bad.

_____ Lindbergh was too young to fly.

_____ The plane was too small to cross the ocean.

_____ Lindbergh was not a good student in school.

_____ The trip was too long.

Your ideas: _____

Lindbergh Did It!

Paris Express News—May 27, 1927

1   PARIS, FRANCE—One week ago, Charles Lindbergh was just a **handsome**, 25-year-old airmail **pilot** from a small town in the United States. Today he is the most famous man in the world and the most important man in the history of flying.

2   Last week, Lindbergh **flew** solo from New York to France. He was the first person to fly non-stop across the Atlantic Ocean alone. He also **set the record** for the longest non-stop **flight**.

3   Lindbergh **took off** on his historic flight on May 20th at 7:52 A.M. People called him "The Flying Fool." On that day, other pilots in the **contest** waited in New York because the weather was bad. Lindbergh did not wait. He took five sandwiches, a bottle of water, a notebook, a pen, and a compass. He didn't even have a radio. All he heard was the sound of the wind and the noise from the engine of the plane. He was in the air all alone with his thoughts, his hopes, and his fears.

4   After 3,610 miles, 33 hours and 30 minutes, and no sleep, Lindbergh **landed** in Paris on May 21st. At that moment, his life changed forever. There were 150,000 excited people waiting to greet him. The international **media** were also there. Photographers and newspaper reporters wanted to be the first to tell the story about Lindbergh. When he got out of his plane and saw all the excitement, he knew that his life would never be the same again.

5   When he began this dangerous flight, he was a quiet young man from a quiet town. This morning, "Lucky Lindy" left Paris as an international **hero**.

◀ **READ FOR MAIN IDEAS**

Circle the answer that best completes each sentence.

1. In 1927, Lindbergh set the record for the _____ non-stop flight.
   a. first   **b.** longest   **c.** highest

2. He was the first person to fly non-stop from _____.
   a. France to the U.S.   **b.** the U.S. to France   **c.** New York to San Diego

(continued on next page)

3. The people waiting in Paris were very _____.

    a. excited   **b.** quiet   **c.** confused

4. Because of his historic flight, Lindbergh became very _____.

    a. handsome   **b.** lucky   **c.** famous

◖ READ FOR DETAILS

Answer each question using one of the numbers from the box. Write your answers in complete sentences.

150,000	3,610	7:52	one	the 21st
~~25~~	33½	five	the 20th	

1. How old was Lindbergh when he flew across the Atlantic?

    <u>Lindbergh was 25 years old when he flew across the Atlantic.</u>

2. On what date did he take off from New York?

_____

3. At what time in the morning did he take off from New York?

_____

4. How many people were on Lindbergh's plane when he flew across the Atlantic?

_____

5. How many miles was Lindbergh's flight?

_____

6. For how many hours was he in the air?

_____

7. How many sandwiches did he bring on his trip?

_____

8. On what date did he land in Paris?

_____

9. About how many people greeted him when he arrived in Paris?

_____

◖ MAKE INFERENCES

Read "Lindbergh Did It!" again, and answer the question. First, discuss your ideas in a small group. Then write at least two reasons. Share your sentences with your group.

Why did Lindbergh fly across the Atlantic?

1. _____

2. _____

◖ EXPRESS OPINIONS

What kind of person was Lindbergh? Work with a partner and choose one word to describe Lindbergh. Talk about why. Then share your choice with the class.

simple

loyal

controversial

independent

adventurous

talkative

your idea: _____

1 *After his historic flight, Lindbergh was very famous. The media followed him everywhere. Read the timeline of his life.*

CHARLES LINDBERGH'S LIFE

Dates	What Happened?
May 21, 1927	"Lucky Lindy" landed in Paris at 10:21 P.M.
May 21–31, 1927	He visited European presidents, kings, and queens.
June 11, 1927	He met the U.S. president in Washington, D.C.
June 13, 1927	He received $25,000 from Raymond Orteig.
July–Dec. 1927	He flew to 82 U.S. cities in 48 states and Latin America on a "friendship tour" in the *Spirit of St. Louis*.
Jan. 28, 1928	*Time* magazine named him "Man of the Year."
May 27, 1929	Lindbergh married Anne Morrow.
March 2, 1932	Someone kidnapped[1] his first child, Charles Jr.
April 1935	Lindbergh invented an "artificial heart."
Dec. 21, 1935	Lindbergh, his wife, and their second son, Jon, moved to England to protect themselves from the media.
Late 1930s–early 1940s	He visited airplane factories in Germany and other countries. People also called him "anti-American" and "a Nazi."
1954	He won the Pulitzer Prize for *The Spirit of St. Louis*, a book about his flight.
Late 1960s–early 1970s	He became an environmentalist. He worked to protect nature and animals in Africa, Asia, and the U.S.
Aug. 26, 1974	He died of cancer in Maui, Hawaii, at the age of 72.

[1] **kidnap** (v): to take someone away illegally and ask for money for returning him or her; a *kidnapper* (n): a person who kidnaps someone

2 *Work with a partner. Charles Lindbergh was not a simple man. He had many different jobs and responsibilities. Look at Reading Two again. Then, on a piece of paper, make a list of Lindbergh's jobs and responsibilities.*

Examples

He was a pilot.

He was a husband.

◀ STEP 1: Organize

Look at Readings One and Two again. What were the high points and low points in Lindbergh's life? Write your answers. Then discuss your answers with the class.

HIGH POINTS	LOW POINTS
He set flying records.	His first son was kidnapped.

◀ STEP 2: Synthesize

Imagine you are Lindbergh. You are writing in your personal diary. Which was the best (highest) point in your life? Which was the worst (lowest)? Say why.

Today the family was here for dinner. It was nice to see everybody. My grandchild Kristina asked me about the "highest" and "lowest" points in my life. I told her that I needed to think about it a little.

So, let's see . . .

The highest point was when (I) _____ because

_____

_____

The lowest point was when (I) _____ because

_____

_____

Maybe I'll call Kristina tomorrow and tell her this . . .

③ FOCUS ON WRITING

Ⓐ VOCABULARY

◖ REVIEW

Read the story about Amelia Earhart. Choose the words that complete the sentences.

Amelia Earhart (1897–1937) was a

_____pilot_____. She became interested
　　1. (pilot / writer)

in flying while working in Canada during

World War I. She started flying in 1922.

In 1928, Earhart _____
　　　　　　　　　　2. (flew / fly)

across the Atlantic Ocean. She was the first

woman to do this. But Earhart was not the

pilot. She was only a passenger.

This _____ made her
　　　3. (flight / contest)

very famous. She was a _____
　　　　　　　　　　　4. (pilot / hero)

to many women and girls. People _____ her "Lady Lindy."
　　　　　　　　　　　　　5. (married / called)

Then, in 1932, she _____ another record. She became the
　　　　　　　　　　　6. (set / flew)

first woman to fly solo across the Atlantic. She _____ from
　　　　　　　　　　　　　　　　　　　　　7. (took off / landed)

Harbour Grace, Newfoundland, and _____ near Londonderry,
　　　　　　　　　　　　　　　　　8. (took off / landed)

Ireland.

In 1935, she became the first person to _____ solo from
　　　　　　　　　　　　　　　　　　　　9. (flew / fly)

Hawaii to California.

In 1937, Earhart and another pilot, Fred Noonan, tried to fly around the

world. Their plane was lost in the Pacific Ocean.

No one knows what happened. It's a mystery. Even today there are stories

in the _____ about Earhart and her mysterious last flight.
　　　10. (media / planes)

A *synonym* is a word that has a similar meaning to another word.

The **price** of the *Spirit of St. Louis* was $10,580.

The **cost** of the *Spirit of St. Louis* was $10,580.

The plane was **built** in San Diego, California.

The plane was **constructed** in San Diego, California.

Read each sentence. Change the underlined word to a synonym from Reading One on page 135. Follow the example.

1. Lindbergh ~~departed~~ *took off* from New York on May 20, 1927.

2. The *Spirit of St. Louis* arrived in France on May 21, 1927.

3. He flew across the Atlantic alone.

4. Lindbergh was a good-looking man.

5. Lindbergh won the competition that Orteig started in 1919.

6. The press gave Lindbergh a lot of attention in the newspapers and on the radio.

7. Lindbergh became well known all over the world.

8. His historic trip changed his life.

9. Amelia Earhart was another famous flier.

◖ CREATE

Terry took a trip to London. When she arrived, she was very tired. At the hotel, she quickly wrote some notes in her travel diary. Look at her notes. Then imagine you are Terry. Write about the trip in complete sentences on the next page. Use the vocabulary from Review and Expand.

- This morning: went to the airport, was early
- Multi-World Airlines Flight 504 from Newark Airport
- Captain Johnson (handsome!) and flight attendants—very nice
- Famous movie star on the plane. Reporters waiting in London.
- 7 hours (not fast, bad weather)
- This evening: London's Heathrow Airport
- To my hotel by taxi

Dear Diary:

This morning I went to the airport. I waited for one hour. Then they called my flight. _____

_____

_____

_____

_____

_____

_____

_____

B GRAMMAR: The Simple Past

1 *Read the paragraphs. Underline the simple past verbs. Then answer the questions.*

On March 1, 1932, someone <u>kidnapped</u> Charles and Anne Lindbergh's baby. The kidnapper left a note in the baby's bedroom. In the note, the kidnapper asked for $50,000. Lindbergh paid the money. Unfortunately, on May 12, 1932, someone found the baby. The baby was dead.

In 1935, the police arrested Bruno Richard Hauptmann. Hauptmann said, "I didn't do it!" Many people did not believe him. Hauptmann died in the electric chair[1] on April 2, 1936. Today, some people believe that Hauptmann did not kidnap the Lindbergh baby.

1. Which past tense verbs are "regular"? Make a list. (*Hint:* They end in -*ed*.)

2. Which past tense verbs are "irregular"? Make a list.

3. How do you form the simple past in negative sentences for regular verbs?

---

[1] **electric chair:** a chair that uses electricity to kill people as punishment for a crime

THE SIMPLE PAST

1. Use the **simple past tense** to talk about actions completed in the past.

People **called** Lindbergh "The Flying Fool."

2. To form the simple past tense:

For regular verbs, **add -ed** to the base form.

If the base form ends in e, **add only -d**.

If the base verb ends in a consonant followed by the letter y, **change the y to i, then add -ed**.

If the base form ends with consonant-vowel-consonant, **double the last consonant, then add -ed**.

Base Form	Simple Past
land	land**ed**
return	return**ed**
receive	receive**d**
live	live**d**
marry	marr**ied**
try	tr**ied**
kidnap	kidna**pped**
stop	sto**pped**

3. Many verbs have irregular forms.

NOTE: The simple past tense of *be* is *was* or *were*, and the simple past tense of *have* is *had*.

become	**became**
do	**did**
fly	**flew**
go	**went**
take	**took**
think	**thought**

4. To make negative statements, use:

    didn't (did not) **+ the base form**

Lindbergh **didn't have** a radio with him.

5. To ask *wh-* questions, use:

    Wh- word **+** *did* **+ subject + base form**

NOTE: If you do not know the subject of the question, do not use *did*.

When did Earhart disappear?

[subject]
Who kidnapped the Lindberghs' baby?

What happened to the Lindberghs' baby?

6. To ask *yes / no* questions, use:

    Did **+ subject + base form**

Did Lindbergh win Orteig's contest?

2 *Complete the paragraphs with the simple past tense form of the verbs.*

Raymond Orteig _____started_____ the flying contest for two reasons.
1. (start)

First, Orteig _____ to build friendship between the United
2. (want)

States and France. He also _____ people to become more
3. (want)

interested in flying.

Five planes _____ to cross the Atlantic during the 1920s,
4. (try)

but no one _____ successful. The flight _____ very
5. (be)   **6. (be)**

dangerous. Six men _____ trying to win the contest. Finally,
7. (die)

Lindbergh _____ it. After Lindbergh _____ in
8. (do)   **9. (arrive)**

Paris, people _____ him a hero. Later, he _____
10. (call)   **11. (become)**

one of the most famous men in the world.

As a boy, Lindbergh _____ very independent. As an adult,
12. (be)

he _____. He _____ strong opinions. Lindbergh
13. (not / change)   **14. (have)**

_____ really anti-American. He _____ the United
15. (not / be)   **16. (not / want)**

States to enter World War II. He _____ that Germany
17. (think)

_____ too strong. Many people _____ with his
18. (be)   **19. (not / agree)**

opinions. At that time, they _____ Lindbergh
20. (not / think)

_____ a hero at all.
21. (be)

144   UNIT 7

3 *Write questions about Charles Lindbergh. Write three* **yes / no** *questions and three* **wh-** *questions in the simple past. Then share your questions with the class.*

Example

    Did Charles and Anne Lindbergh have more than one child?

1. _____

2. _____

3. _____

Example

    Why did Lindbergh and his family move to England in 1935?

4. _____

5. _____

6. _____

C WRITING

In this unit, you read about Charles Lindbergh and his first solo, non-stop flight across the Atlantic Ocean.

You are going to **write a paragraph about a trip you remember**. Write about the high point and the low point of the trip. Use the vocabulary and grammar from the unit.*

PREPARE TO WRITE: Making a Timeline

To help you write about your trip, you are going to make a timeline as a prewriting activity. There are different kinds of timelines. The travel diary on page 146 is one kind. Look at page 138 for another example.

1 *Make a list of trips you remember. Think about trips you took for vacation, business, or school. They can be trips you enjoyed or trips you didn't enjoy.*

Example

Trips	Alaska
beach	honeymoon
Grandmother's house	London

---

*For Alternative Writing Topics, see page 150. These topics can be used in place of the writing topic for this unit or as homework. The alternative topics relate to the theme of the unit, but may not target the same grammar or rhetorical structures taught in the unit.

2 *Choose one memorable trip from your list to write about. Then look at the travel diary of a vacation in August 2007.*

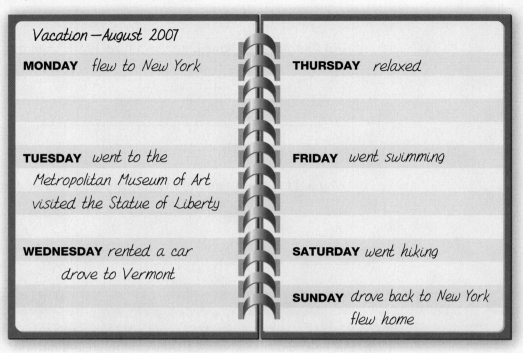

Vacation—August 2007

MONDAY flew to New York

TUESDAY went to the Metropolitan Museum of Art visited the Statue of Liberty

WEDNESDAY rented a car drove to Vermont

THURSDAY relaxed

FRIDAY went swimming

SATURDAY went hiking

SUNDAY drove back to New York flew home

3 *Make a timeline of your trip on a separate piece of paper.*

◀ **WRITE: An Autobiography**

An **autobiography** is a story about the writer. The writer tells the story in time order starting with the first event and ending with the last event.

1 *The sentences are not in order. Look back at the travel diary in Prepare to Write, Exercise 2. Put the sentences in order. Number them from 1 to 8.*

_____ Then we drove to New York City on Sunday morning.

_____ Finally, we flew home on Sunday night.

_____ It was a great vacation.

__1__ My husband and I had a wonderful honeymoon trip four years ago.

_____ On Wednesday, we rented a car and drove to Vermont.

_____ We went swimming and hiking, and we relaxed.

_____ The next day, we went to the Metropolitan Museum of Art and the Statue of Liberty.

_____ First, we flew to New York City on Monday.

2 Now write the sentences in paragraph form in your notebook.

3 Look at the travel diary and complete the paragraph. Put a check (✓) next to the topic sentence.

Five years ago, my friend and I had a terrible vacation in Florida.

Everything went wrong. First, we _____. Then we
                                                    1.

_____. We arrived in Florida with no clothes, so we
               2.

_____. Next, it _____ for two
          3.   4.

days. Finally, it stopped raining, and we _____. Then
                                                           5.

we _____ the next day. It was a terrible vacation.
                6.

4 Write your first draft. Write a paragraph about a memorable trip. Put the events in time order. Don't worry about the grammar. Just try to make your ideas clear.

Time order words show the order of events. They help your reader understand your story. Time order words usually come at the beginning of a sentence.

I went hiking with my brother last week.

First, we put on our new hiking shoes.

Then we put our food and water in our backpacks.

Next, my brother gave me his food because his backpack was too heavy.

Later, he gave me his water because his backpack was still too heavy.

Finally, we got to the top of the mountain.

Hiking is fun, but not with my brother!

Other time words or expressions tell *when* or *how long*:

Last year, I went to New York. (*last week, last month, yesterday*)

We left **the next day.** (*the next week, the next month, the next year*)

I went to New York **two years ago.** (*two months ago, two weeks ago, two days ago*)

On Wednesday, we drove to New Hampshire. (*on Tuesday, on Friday, on Saturday*)

We went to Florida **for a week.** (*for an hour, for a month, for a year*)

1 *Look back at the paragraph about the trip to Florida in Write, Exercise 3, on page 147. Underline the time order words or other time words.*

2 *Look at the travel diary. Complete the paragraph with the time order words or other time words from the box. Capitalize the words if necessary.*

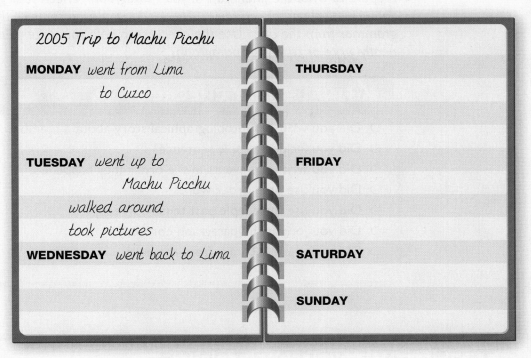

2005 Trip to Machu Picchu

MONDAY *went from Lima to Cuzco*

TUESDAY *went up to Machu Picchu*
walked around
took pictures

WEDNESDAY *went back to Lima*

THURSDAY

FRIDAY

SATURDAY

SUNDAY

| the next day | ~~on Monday~~ | for about six hours | finally |

In 2005, my sister and I had a wonderful visit to Machu Picchu, the old Inca city in Peru. ___On Monday___, we went from Lima to Cuzco.

1.

_____, we went up the mountain to Machu Picchu. We walked

2.

around and took pictures _____. We were really tired, but it was

3.

very interesting. We learned about the Incan people. _____, we

4.

went back to Lima on Wednesday. We want to visit again soon.

3 *Look at the first draft of your paragraph. Underline the time order words. Is the order of events clear? Add or change time order words to make your paragraph clear.*

Prepare to write the final draft of your paragraph. Check your grammar, spelling, capitalization, and punctuation. Check that you used some of the vocabulary and grammar from the unit. Use the checklist to help you write your final draft. Then neatly write or type your paragraph.

✓ FINAL DRAFT CHECKLIST

❍ Did you write an autobiographical story about a memorable trip?

❍ Did you include a topic sentence?

❍ Did you write the events in the order they happened?

❍ Did you use time order words?

❍ Did you use the simple past tense correctly?

❍ Did you format the paragraph correctly?

❍ Did you use vocabulary from the unit?

ALTERNATIVE WRITING TOPICS

Write about one of the topics. Use the vocabulary and grammar from the unit.

1. Write a paragraph about a time when your life changed in a good way or in a bad way. What happened? How did you deal with the change? Use simple past verbs and time order words and expressions.

2. Think about Charles Lindbergh's life. Then imagine that you are Charles Lindbergh. It is June 1974, and you are near the end of your life. Write a letter to your family. Tell them about some of the high points and low points of your life. Use simple past verbs and time order words and expressions in your letter.

3. The artist Andy Warhol said that everyone has "15 minutes of fame." Write a paragraph about someone you know who became famous for a little while. What happened? Did the person change? Use simple past verbs and time order words and expressions.

RESEARCH TOPICS, see page 221.

Are We There Yet?

①FOCUS ON THE TOPIC

A PREDICT

Look at the picture. Discuss the question with the class.

The man is stuck (not moving) in traffic. How does he feel? Explain.

Think of a time you were stuck in traffic (in a car, on a bus, on a plane, etc.). Answer the questions. Then ask three classmates these questions. Write their answers.

	YOU	STUDENT 1	STUDENT 2	STUDENT 3
Where were you?				
Where were you going?				
Were you in a car, on a bus, or somewhere else?				
How long were you stuck there?				
What did you do in the car (on the bus, on the plane, etc.)?				
How did you feel?				

1 *Sarah works for the New York City government. She is in her car and sends an e-mail message to her co-worker, Emily. Read her e-mail. Then match each boldfaced word or phrase to its definition. Write the word or phrase on the line.*

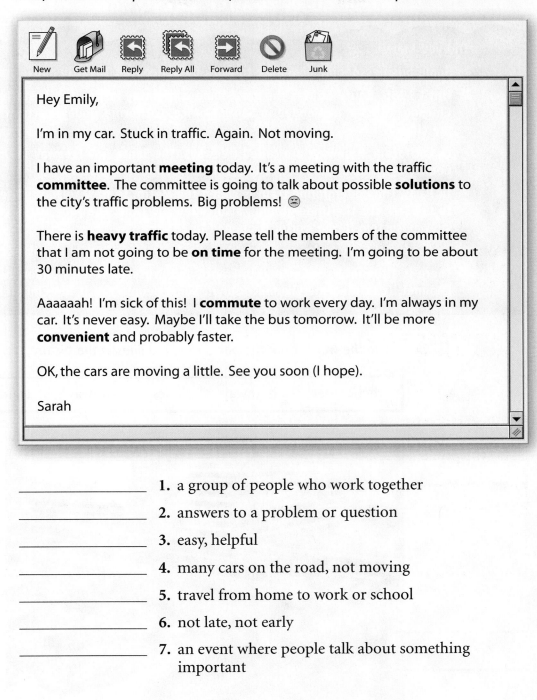

New	Get Mail	Reply	Reply All	Forward	Delete	Junk

Hey Emily,

I'm in my car. Stuck in traffic. Again. Not moving.

I have an important **meeting** today. It's a meeting with the traffic **committee**. The committee is going to talk about possible **solutions** to the city's traffic problems. Big problems! ☹

There is **heavy traffic** today. Please tell the members of the committee that I am not going to be **on time** for the meeting. I'm going to be about 30 minutes late.

Aaaaaah! I'm sick of this! I **commute** to work every day. I'm always in my car. It's never easy. Maybe I'll take the bus tomorrow. It'll be more **convenient** and probably faster.

OK, the cars are moving a little. See you soon (I hope).

Sarah

_____ **1.** a group of people who work together

_____ **2.** answers to a problem or question

_____ **3.** easy, helpful

_____ **4.** many cars on the road, not moving

_____ **5.** travel from home to work or school

_____ **6.** not late, not early

_____ **7.** an event where people talk about something important

2 *Read "Travel Facts."*

TRAVEL FACTS

Did you know . . . ?

▶ Some businesspeople commute to work by **helicopter.** They fly above the traffic.

▶ Until 1985, Route 66 was the most famous **highway** in the U.S. It started in Chicago, Illinois, and ended in Santa Monica, California. Today, parts of Route 66 are closed.

▶ In California, highways are called freeways. The Santa Ana Freeway in Orange County is 12 **lanes** across. It's the widest freeway in the state.

▶ In Paris, the underground train is called the Metro. In New York, it's the **subway.** In London, it's the Underground, also called the Tube. The Tube is the oldest subway system in the world. It opened in 1863.

▶ To see the U.S. by **train**, most people take Amtrak, the national rail system.

▶ There is a **tunnel** from England to France and Brussels. It goes under the English Channel. It's called the Channel Tunnel. Some people call it the Chunnel.

3 *Write the words from the box on the red lines in the picture.*

helicopter	highway	lanes	subway	train	tunnel

2 FOCUS ON READING

You are going to read a memo about traffic. Before you read, think about traffic. Check (✓) the words you think you will see in the memo. Share your answers with the class. Then read the memo.

_____ avoid

_____ expert

_____ increase

_____ pilot

_____ problem

_____ the Internet

New	Get Mail	Reply	Reply All	Forward	Delete	Junk

From: RafaelTorres@NYCTraffic.gov
To: Traffic **Solutions Committee**, New York, NY
Subject: Our next **meeting**

This committee wants to find a solution to the traffic problem in New York City. Last month, I studied solutions from other cities around the world. Please read this information before our next meeting.

Traffic Solutions in the United States

- Seattle, Washington, has bike **lanes** on many streets. Commuters don't worry about **heavy traffic**, and they feel healthy because they ride their bikes.

- Atlanta, Georgia, has an online traffic map. The map shows commuters where there is heavy traffic. Drivers can check the traffic on their computers at home. People need a little extra time in the morning to check the online map.

- The State of Connecticut has a "Deduct-a-Ride" program. Commuters save money if they don't use their cars. They pay lower taxes when they use public buses and **trains**. But, some people still have to drive because they do not work near public transportation.

(continued on next page)

- Washington, D.C., has high-occupancy vehicle (HOV) lanes. HOV lanes are for cars with three or more people. Traffic moves much faster in HOV lanes because there are fewer cars. Unfortunately, some people have to drive to work alone because they do not live near co-workers.
- Boston, Massachusetts, had its "Big Dig" project. The project put part of I-93, the main **highway**, in a **tunnel** under the city. The area is beautiful. They planned $2.8 billion for the Big Dig. By the end, however, it cost more than $14.6 billion. People in Massachusetts are not happy about that.

Traffic Solutions Internationally

- In São Paulo, Brazil, some people use **helicopters** to get around the city. Taking a helicopter is fast and easy. But most people can't do this because helicopters are very expensive.
- Manila, Philippines, has a commuter train along the center of a major highway. Instead of driving, people ride the train. This is **convenient** for people who live near the train.
- Bangkok, Thailand, has a skytrain. It's like the **subway** but not underground. It is about 14 miles (23 km) long. It is clean, fast, and **on time**. Traffic in Bangkok is a little better now.
- London and Singapore have a traffic tax for people who drive in the center of the city. The tax is about $8 per car. It works. There is less traffic, and people use public transportation more. Some people say it is not fair. They say that only people with a lot of money can drive in the city because the tax is expensive.

Can New York use any of these solutions? Please think about this information carefully. We will discuss it at our next meeting on Monday at 10:00 A.M.

See you then.
Rafael

◖ **READ FOR MAIN IDEAS**

Read the sentences. Check (✓) the main idea of Mr. Torres' memo.

Mr. Torres wants the committee to . . .

_____ **1.** visit the cities in his report.

_____ **2.** think about the solutions in these cities.

_____ **3.** take public transportation more often.

◖ READ FOR DETAILS

Match the place on the left with the traffic solution on the right.

Places

			Solutions
_e_	**1.** Seattle, WA		**a.** helicopters
____	**2.** Atlanta, GA		**b.** a traffic tax
____	**3.** Connecticut		**c.** Deduct-a-Ride
____	**4.** Washington, D.C.		**d.** an online traffic map
____	**5.** Boston, MA		**e.** bike lanes
____	**6.** São Paulo, Brazil		**f.** a commuter train along the highway
____	**7.** Manila, Philippines		**g.** a skytrain
____	**8.** Bangkok, Thailand		**h.** HOV lanes
____	**9.** London and Singapore		**i.** a tunnel for a highway under the city

◖ MAKE INFERENCES

1 *Read Mr. Torres' memo again. Which three solutions do you think are Mr. Torres' favorites? Choose from the box. Explain.*

bicycle lanes	helicopters	skytrain
commuter train along the highway	HOV lanes	traffic tax
Deduct-a-Ride program	online traffic map	tunnels

1. _____

2. _____

3. _____

2 *Discuss your answers to Exercise 1 with the class. Complete the sentences.*

Mr. Torres probably likes the idea of having _____

(solution)

because _____.

(reason)

Mr. Torres probably doesn't like the idea of having

_____ because _____.

(solution)   (reason)

◖ EXPRESS OPINIONS

1 *In your opinion, what is the best solution for New York? Put the choices in order from 1–9. Number 1 is the best solution.*

____ bicycle lanes

____ commuter train along the highway

____ Deduct-a-Ride program

____ helicopters

____ HOV lanes

____ online traffic map

____ skytrain

____ traffic tax

____ tunnels

2 *Discuss your choices with a partner. Here are some ways to explain your choices.*

I think this is a good choice because _____.

- it/they will be good for the environment
- people will have a shorter commute
- it/they will be convenient
- it/they will be faster
- (your own answer)

1 *Read the article.*

Transit Talk: New Yorkers Talk Traffic, Mayor in the Slow Lane[1]

Fifty-nine percent of New Yorkers think that the mayor is not doing a good job with the city's traffic problems. They think he is a good mayor, but 79 percent of New Yorkers think traffic is a problem.

This information comes from telephone interviews with 800 New Yorkers. The responses show that New York City residents have strong opinions about the city's traffic.

Here are some details:

- 73 percent believe that there are too many trucks on city streets.
- 71 percent believe that roads and bridges are in poor condition.
- 70 percent believe that streets are not safe for pedestrians to walk on.
- 43 percent think that streets are not safe for bicyclists to ride on.
- 33 percent think that public buses move too slowly.
- 50 percent say that pollution[2] from traffic—including noise—is a serious problem.

New Yorkers want the mayor to find solutions to the city's traffic problems.

----

[1] **About the survey:** The Tri-State Transportation Campaign is an independent, non-profit policy and advocacy group promoting environmentally friendly transportation policies in the New York metropolitan region. Michaels Opinion Research, Inc., is a New York City-based public opinion research and consulting firm.
http://www.tstc.org/press/2006/080706_NYCOpinion.html

[2] **pollution** (n): dirty or dangerous air, water, or earth; *pollute* (v)

2 *Write **T** (true) or **F** (false).*

_____ 1. In general, the mayor is popular.

_____ 2. New Yorkers want the mayor to do something about the city's traffic problems.

◖ **STEP 1: Organize**

Think about New York's problems in Reading Two and the solutions in Reading One. Which solutions might work for each problem? Write the solutions from the box in the chart. More than one answer is possible.

bike lanes	helicopter	sky train	tunnel under city
Deduct-a-Ride	online traffic map	traffic tax	

TRAFFIC PROBLEMS IN NEW YORK CITY	POSSIBLE SOLUTIONS
Trucks	
Poor conditions of roads and bridges	
Streets not safe for pedestrians	
Streets not safe for bicyclists	
Slow buses	
Pollution, including noise	

◖ **STEP 2: Synthesize**

1 *Work with a partner. One student is Rafael Torres, and the other the mayor of New York. Complete the interview between Torres (T) and the mayor (M). Use the information from the readings. Do not give your own opinion.*

T: Mr. Mayor, as you know, there are serious traffic problems in this city. I have data to show you.

M: Yes, I know. What did the poll say?

T: Well, one big problem is . . .

M: OK, to solve that problem I want to . . .

2 *Change roles and repeat Exercise 1 with a different problem and solution.*

3 *Present one of your conversations to the class.*

3 FOCUS ON WRITING

A VOCABULARY

REVIEW

Complete the paragraph with the words and phrases from the box. Use each word only once.

committee	heavy traffic	on time	solutions
commute	helicopter	pedestrians	subway
convenient	meetings	~~residents~~	

Bangkok

Most _____residents_____ of **1.** Bangkok stay relaxed in traffic. "We don't get upset," said one woman. "Getting angry or upset will not change anything. _____ is a part **2.** of life here." People in Bangkok plan on slow-moving traffic. Families often _____ together. They **3.** leave home at 5:30 A.M. to get to school and to work _____. Some **4.** commuters work in their cars while they sit in traffic. Employers still get angry when employees are late for work. They are sometimes late for _____ because of the traffic. The skytrain helps a little, and the underground **5.** _____ does too. They are very _____ for many people. But a special **6.** **7.** _____ in the Bangkok city government is looking for more _____ to **8.** **9.** the traffic problems. The members of the committee do not want Bangkok's traffic problem to increase. _____ do not worry about traffic. They just walk. **10.**

Use *take*, *get*, and *go* to talk about commuting or traveling.

Take is about **time**. *Get* is similar to *arrive*.	Does it **take** (you) a long time to **get** home from school?
	  No, it doesn't **take** (me) long (a long time).
	
	How long does it **take** (you) to **get** home?
	  It **takes** (me) about 15 minutes.

Take is also about *how* you go.	How do you **get** there? Do you **take** the bus?
	  No, I don't **take** the bus.
	  No, I don't. I walk.

Go is similar to *travel*.	I **go** by car (bus, subway, skytrain, train). I live a few miles away.

1 *Complete the paragraph with* **take, get,** *or* **go.** *Use the correct form of the verb.*

I live in New York City, but I work outside the city. It _____ me
                                                                1.
about 90 minutes to _____ home from work. I walk from my office to the
                          2.
Metro-North train station. It _____ about three minutes. I _____ the
                                      3.   4.
Metro-North train to Grand Central Station at 42nd Street in New York City.
That trip _____ about 35 minutes. From Grand Central I _____ the
                 5.   6.
Shuttle train across to Times Square. Then I _____ the "1" Train to 23rd
                                                      7.
Street. Then I walk from the subway to my apartment. When I _____
                                                                          8.
home, I relax. I don't drive because traffic is heavy. If I _____ by car, the
                                                                    9.
trip _____ longer. So, for now, I will continue to _____ by train.
         10.   11.

2 *Answer the questions about yourself.*

1. Does it take you a long time to get home after school or work?

_____

_____

2. How long does it take you to get home?

_____

_____

3. How do you usually get home?

_____

_____

4. How do you go to work or school each day?

_____

_____

(CREATE

Write three questions to ask your partner. Ask about his or her commute from home to school or work. Use the vocabulary from Review and Expand.

1. _____

_____

2. _____

_____

3. _____

_____

Write your partner's answers. Then report to the class.

1. _____

_____

2. _____

_____

3. _____

_____

1 *Work with a partner. Say these words to each other. Count the number of syllables in each word. For example, the word* **easy** *has two syllables (ea • sy). The word* **small** *has only one syllable. Write the number of syllables on the line.*

_1_   **a.** big

_____   **b.** busy

_____   **c.** expensive

_____   **d.** noisy

_____   **e.** old

COMPARATIVE ADJECTIVES	
1. Use **comparative adjectives** to compare two people, places, or things.	My sister is **taller** than my brother. The bookstore is **larger** than the video store.
2. For adjectives with one syllable, **add -er**.	The subway is big**ger**. The subway is cheap**er**. An exception: *fun / more fun*

3. For adjectives with two or more syllables, use *more + adjective*.	The Underground is **more expensive**.
	
	 Some exceptions:
	
	   *quiet / quiet**er***
	
	   *simple / simpl**er***

4. For adjectives with two syllables that end in y, **change y to i and add -er**.	The subway is bus**ier**.
5. Use *than* when you are comparing two things in one sentence.	The Underground is more expensive *than* the subway. The subway is busier *than* the Underground.

2 With your partner, read this information about the New York City subway and London's underground. Then write the answers in complete sentences. Follow the example.

	MTA New York City Subway	London Underground
Stations	468	255
Riders	4.8 million per day	3 million per day
Employees	26,000	12,560
Cost (fares)	U.S. $2.00	U.S. $1.00–$5.85
Hours open each day	24	19 (M–Sa), 15 (Su)
Year opened	1904	1863

1. Which is bigger, the New York City subway or the London Underground?

    The New York City subway is bigger than the London Underground.

2. Which is busier?

    _____

3. Which is more expensive to ride?

    _____

4. Which is probably noisier?

    _____

5. Which is older?

    _____

3 *Work with a partner. Take turns asking questions about driving a car and walking to school or work. Write your partner's answers. Use the comparative form of the adjectives in parentheses. Then write a short paragraph about your partner's opinion.*

Your question: Which is faster, driving a car or walking?

Your partner's answers:

1. ___Driving a car is faster than walking._____ (fast)

2. _____ (cheap)

3. _____ (convenient)

4. _____ (fun)

5. _____ (dangerous)

6. _____ (quiet)

7. _____ (healthy)

8. _____ (relaxing)

Your partner's opinion:

In general, _____ thinks _____ is
         (your partner's name)   (driving a car/walking)

better than _____ because _____
                                      (driving a car/walking)

_____

C WRITING

In this unit, you read about traffic problems and possible solutions.

You are going to **write a paragraph about the best way for you to get from your home to school or work.** Give three reasons why one way is better than another. Use the vocabulary and grammar from the unit.*

◖ PREPARE TO WRITE: Making a Chart

To help you organize your paragraph, you are going to make a chart as a prewriting activity. Making a chart can help you compare two things. For example, you can list good things (advantages) and bad things (disadvantages).

---

*For Alternative Writing Topics, see page 170. These topics can be used in place of the writing topic for this unit or as homework. The alternative topics relate to the theme of the unit, but may not target the same grammar or rhetorical structures taught in the unit.

1 *Read the chart. It shows advantages and disadvantages for two different ways to get to work.*

WAYS TO GET TO WORK	ADVANTAGES	DISADVANTAGES
DRIVING	You don't get wet when it rains. It's cooler to drive in hot weather.	It's slower when there's traffic. It's stressful when traffic is bad. It's hard to find parking. You don't get exercise.
WALKING	You get exercise. It's not stressful. It's faster when there's traffic. You don't have to park the car.	You get wet when it rains. Work shoes are less comfortable for walking.

2 *Choose two ways that you can get to school or work (for example, driving; taking the bus, train, or subway; walking; or riding a bicycle). Make a chart on a separate piece of paper. List the advantages and disadvantages of both ways. Use the questions to help you. Think of your own ideas.*

- Is it more or less convenient?
- Is it more or less comfortable?
- Is it faster or slower?
- Is it more expensive or cheaper?
- Is the traffic lighter or heavier?
- Is it better or worse for the environment?

3 *Look at your chart. Compare the advantages and disadvantages of both ways. Then choose the best way for you to get to work or school.*

WRITE: A Comparison and Contrast Paragraph

> A **comparison and contrast paragraph** describes how two things (or people) are similar and different. In the topic sentence, give your main idea—your answer to the question. Then explain your opinion about how the two things or people are similar and different.

1 *Read the paragraph.*

Walking to work is better than driving to work. One reason is that walking to my job is usually faster than driving. This is because traffic is heavy, and it moves slowly. Another reason is that walking is more enjoyable than driving. I can relax when I walk. I get upset when there is a lot of traffic. The most important reason is that walking is healthier. My office is one mile away from my house. I don't get any exercise when I drive. So, I prefer to walk. Even on rainy days, I take my umbrella, not my car.

2 *Work with a partner. Complete the outline of the paragraph in Exercise 1.*

Topic Sentence (main idea): _Walking is better than driving._ _____

Reason 1: _____

Explanation: _____

Reason 2: _____

Explanation: _____

Reason 3: _____

Explanation: _____

3 *Now, write an outline of your paragraph. Use the ideas in the chart you made in Prepare to Write on page 167. Then use your outline to write the first draft of your paragraph.*

◀ REVISE: Putting Your Reasons in Order

To put your reasons in order, use these transition words and phrases:

First,

In addition,

Finally,

One reason is that

Another reason is that

A second/third/final reason is that

} driving is more comfortable than taking the train.

For more about giving reasons, see Unit 2, *Write*, page 38.

1 *Read the paragraph in Write, Exercise 1, on page 168. Underline the transition words and phrases that introduce reasons.*

2 *Read the list of reasons why flying is better than driving. Then work with a partner. Which are the three best reasons? Check (✓) them.*

Reasons

_____ Flying is better. Driving can take all day.

_____ Flying is more comfortable. You can get up and walk around.

_____ Flight attendants bring you food and drinks. You don't have to stop at a restaurant.

_____ Airplanes are more fun. For example, on many planes you can use the Internet and watch movies.

_____ You can sleep on an airplane, so you are not tired when you get to the place you are going.

3 *Work with a partner. Complete the paragraph with the three best reasons you chose in Exercise 2. Use transition words or phrases to introduce each reason.*

I like flying more than driving. _____

_____

_____

_____

_____

_____ For all these reasons, flying is better than driving.

4 *Look at your paragraph. Add transition words to your paragraph.*

◖ **EDIT: Writing the Final Draft**

Prepare to write the final draft of your paragraph. Check your grammar, spelling, capitalization, and punctuation. Check that you used some of the vocabulary and grammar from the unit. Use the checklist to help you write your final draft. Then neatly write or type your paragraph.

✓ FINAL DRAFT CHECKLIST

- ○ Did you tell the best way for you to get to school or work?
- ○ Did you give three reasons?
- ○ Did you explain your reasons?
- ○ Did you use transition words and phrases?
- ○ Did you use comparative adjectives?
- ○ Did you use vocabulary from the unit?

ALTERNATIVE WRITING TOPICS

Write about one of the topics. Use the vocabulary and grammar from the unit.

1. Write a letter to a local government official. Tell the official about a specific traffic problem in your town or city. Suggest a solution.

2. Which do you prefer when you travel: flying or taking a train? Write a paragraph about your choice. Compare flying and taking a train. Give a reason for your answer.

3. Does traffic change your daily life in any way, good or bad? Write a paragraph about how traffic changes your life.

RESEARCH TOPICS, see page 222.

Full House

①FOCUS ON THE TOPIC

A PREDICT

Look at the picture. Discuss the questions with the class.

1. How many children are there in this family?

2. How old are the children?

3. Do the children look alike?

1 *Look at the picture on page 171 again. The woman in the picture is Ellen Sullivan. Read Ellen's interview with* Family Friendly *magazine.*

FF: How many people are there in your family? What are their names?
ES: There are five people in my family. My husband, Bob, and I have three daughters, Kathryn, Kelly, and Heather.

FF: Are there any multiple births in your family?

ES: Yes, there are. Kelly and Heather are twins. They were born in the same year and on the same day. Kathryn is one year older. Kathryn is behind her father in the picture on page 171.

FF: Where does your family live?
ES: We live in Salem, Massachusetts.

2 *Now write your own answers to the questions in Exercise 1. Then ask a partner. Write your partner's answers.*

Your answers:

1. _____

2. _____

3. _____

Your partner's answers:

1. _____

2. _____

3. _____

Read more of the interview with Ellen Sullivan. Then circle the answer that correctly completes each sentence.

FF: How many children did you want to have?
ES: Well, I wanted three children. I wanted Kathryn to have **siblings**.

FF: After the doctor said, "You are going to have twins," how did you feel?
ES: When I found out I was **pregnant** with twins, I was very surprised. There were no twins in my family before this.

FF: You had one daughter before the twins. Were there any special **challenges** when the twins arrived?
ES: Well, time was a challenge. With three little kids I was very busy. Another challenge was money. Luckily, friends and family helped us. They helped around the house. They also **donated** extra clothes and toys. My husband and I were very thankful for the support.

FF: Does your older daughter ever feel **jealous**?
ES: Not anymore. When they were little, she felt a little jealous because the twins got a lot of attention. But she knows she is **unique**, and we love her very much.

FF: What's the best thing about living in your house?
ES: There is usually a lot of **laughter**. My husband tells a lot of jokes. We laugh a lot.

1. If a child has **siblings,** she has _____.
   a. a mother and father
   b. brothers and sisters

2. If a woman is **pregnant,** she is going to _____.
   a. have a baby
   b. take a long vacation

3. A **challenge** is something _____.
   a. difficult you need to do
   b. fun you often do

4. If you **donated** something, you _____.
   a. received something because you needed help
   b. gave something to someone who needed help

5. When you are **jealous,** you feel _____.
   a. unhappy because someone is getting something you want
   b. thankful because you are getting something you want

6. Something that is **unique** is _____.
   a. special because there is only one
   b. valuable because it is very old

7. When you hear **laughter,** someone probably said something _____.
   a. interesting
   b. funny

A READING ONE: Full House

1 *Before you read, look at the chart. Answer the questions.*

CHILDREN BORN IN THE UNITED STATES 2000–2005						
Children	2000	2001	2002	2003	2004	2005
Single births	3,932,573	3,897,216	3,889,191	3,953,622	3,972,558	3,998,855
Twins	118,916	121,246	125,134	128,665	_____	133,122
Triplets	6,742	6,885	6,898	7,110	6,750	_____
Quadruplets	506	501	434	_____	439	418
Quintuplets and Sextuplets	77	85	69	85	86	68
Total multiple births	126,241	_____	132,535	136,328	139,494	139,816
Total births	_____	4,025,933	4,021,726	4,089,950	4,112,052	4,138,349

1. How many births were there in 2000?

2. How many multiple births were there in 2001?

3. How many quadruplets were born in 2003?

4. How many twins were born in 2004?

5. How many triplets were born in 2005?

6. Is the number of total births going up or going down?

2 *The title of this newspaper article is* Full House. *What do you think this story is about?*

FULL HOUSE

1 *Des Moines, Iowa—(CCN)* On November 18, 1997, there were about 3,400 people in Carlisle, Iowa. The next day, that number increased to 3,407. It was a historic day.

2 Kenny and Bobbi McCaughey (pronounced ma·'koy) had one daughter, Mikayla, but they wanted her to have **siblings**. Unfortunately, Bobbi was having trouble getting **pregnant**. Bobbi's doctor asked, "Do you want to try fertility drugs?"[1]

3 The doctor explained the risks of fertility drugs: The baby might not be healthy, or Bobbi might have a multiple birth. Kenny and Bobbi talked to each other. Then they decided to take the risk.

4 After one month, they visited the doctor again. He told Bobbi, "You are going to have *seven* babies." Everyone was surprised and nervous. The doctor explained, "This is very dangerous." Kenny and Bobbi talked again. Then they said, "OK. They are all our children. We want them."

5 On November 19th Bobbi had the babies—two months early. Forty doctors and nurses helped. In six minutes, Bobbi had four boys and three girls. They were the first living septuplets.

6 When the septuplets were little, the McCaugheys got a lot of support from their family and their church. Seventy volunteers—

eight or nine every day—helped to cook, clean, and take care of the kids.

7 Companies and other generous people also helped. For example:

- Chevrolet®, a car company, **donated** a new van for 15 people.
- Carter's®, a clothing company, donated clothes for five years.
- Gerber® donated baby food.
- Procter & Gamble® donated Pampers® diapers[2]. The family used 150–170 diapers each week.
- The State of Iowa donated a new house with five bedrooms and bathrooms.

Today, more than ten years later, life in the McCaugheys' home is not always easy. There is still a lot of work to do. The kids are sometimes noisy, but there is also a lot

(continued on next page)

---

[1] **fertility drugs:** medicine to help a woman become pregnant

[2] **diaper:**

of **laughter**. But Bobbi and Kenny love all eight children. Each one is **unique**:

- Mikayla is one year older than the septuplets. Sometimes she feels **jealous**, but not often. She is a good big sister.
- Kenny Jr. was the first septuplet. His nickname is "Bert." He is energetic.
- Alexis has the best smile. She likes to listen to violin music in her room.
- Natalie is dramatic. When she was little, she cried about many things. But she is a good girl.
- Kelsey is very friendly. She likes to talk to people. She talks a lot.
- Nathan is shy and likes to laugh. He likes to play with the other kids.
- Brandon likes "army" things. He likes to play outside.
- Joel likes to read. He also thinks about things carefully.

8   Alexis and Nathan have cerebral palsy, a physical problem, so it is difficult for them to walk. But they are still very active.

9   The McCaugheys are famous, but they also have a normal life. After the septuplets were born, Bobbi and Kenny did many interviews. They recorded a CD of bedtime music called *Sweet Dreams*. They wrote a book called *Seven from Heaven*. In 2006, the children recorded a CD of Christmas music. Every December *Ladies' Home Journal*, a magazine, has a story about the McCaugheys.

10   Kenny and Bobbi want their family to be happy and strong. They do their best for their family. If there are **challenges**, they face them together. They also try to spend some time with each other. They have a "date night" every Friday. They are ready for the future.

Primary source: www.lhj.com

3 *Check the prediction you made in Exercise 2.*

◖ READ FOR MAIN IDEAS

*Read each sentence. Write **T** (true) or **F** (false).*

_____ **1.** Sometimes it is dangerous to take fertility drugs.

_____ **2.** Nobody was surprised about the septuplets.

_____ **3.** The McCaugheys had the first living septuplets.

_____ **4.** The septuplets have similar personalities.

Read Full House *again. Then complete the sentences with the correct numbers. Compare your answers with a partner's.*

1. Before the septuplets, the McCaugheys had _____ child.
2. On the day the McCaughey septuplets were born, about _____ people lived in Carlisle, Iowa.
3. She gave birth to the septuplets _____ months early.
4. _____ doctors and nurses helped Bobbi.
5. Kenny and Bobbi have _____ sons and _____ daughters.
6. Mikayla has _____ brothers and _____ sisters.
7. Bobbi gave birth to the septuplets in only _____ minutes.
8. About _____ people can sit in the McCaugheys' van.
9. They got free clothes for _____ years.
10. The McCaugheys used _____ to _____ diapers every week.
11. Their house has _____ bedrooms and _____ bathrooms.
12. _____ of the McCaughey kids have physical problems.

◖ MAKE INFERENCES

Look back at the reading. Then answer the question in complete sentences. Give your reasons.

Do Kenny and Bobbi McCaughey have a strong marriage?

_____

_____

◖ EXPRESS OPINIONS

Work with a partner. Answer the questions.

1. There are eight children in the McCaughey family. What is the best number of children in a family: 1, 2, 3, or more? Why?
2. Mikayla is one year older than the septuplets. The age range between Mikayla and the septuplets is one year. The age range among the septuplets is 0. What do you think is the best age range for kids in a family: 1, 2, 3, or more years? Why?
3. There are girls and boys in the McCaughey family. What do you think is best mix in a family: All girls, boys, or boys and girls? Why?

In 1934, the Dionne quintuplets were born in Ontario, Canada. Multiple births were not common then. In 1997, three of the Dionne sisters wrote a letter to Kenny and Bobbi McCaughey.

The Dionne sisters in 1937

1 *Read the letter on the next page. It is similar to the letter that the Dionnes wrote to the McCaugheys.*

Cécile, Antoinette, and Yvonne Dionne in 1998

November 1997

Dear Mr. and Mrs. McCaughey,

Congratulations on the birth of your beautiful children. We have a very special family, too. We want to tell you our story.

We were born on May 28, 1934, in a small town in Canada. Our family was poor. Our father thought, "Five daughters! If my daughters become famous, I can make a lot of money."

The Ontario government took us away from our family to protect us from our father. Unfortunately, they did not protect us. We lived in a special house called "Quintland." Every day, tourists came to look at us. We had no privacy. Everyone watched us in the news and in our home. We became very famous. The government made a lot of money, but we received very little money or love. We had a very unhappy life.

Today we receive letters of support from people all over the world. We thank them.

We hope your children will receive more respect than we did as children. Multiple births are not for entertainment. They are not a chance to sell products. We hope your children will have happy lives. Please love and protect them always.

Sincerely,

Annette, Cécile, & Yvonne Dionne

2 *Read each sentence. Write **T** (true), **F** (false), or **?** (if the information is not in the reading).*

_____ **1.** The Dionne sisters became very rich.

_____ **2.** The Dionne sisters became very famous.

_____ **3.** The Dionne sisters live in Ontario today.

_____ **4.** The Dionnes want the McCaugheys to protect their children.

◀ STEP 1: Organize

*Review Readings One and Two. Then complete the chart. Write the **pros** (advantages) and **cons** (disadvantages) of having a big family, according to the McCaugheys and the Dionnes.*

HAVING A BIG FAMILY		
	Pros	Cons
The McCaugheys		
The Dionnes		

Imagine you are Bobbi or Kenny McCaughey. Write a letter to the Dionne sisters. Write about your family life. Also tell the Dionnes what you learned from their letter.

Dear Friends,

Thank you, again, for writing to us. The septuplets are ten years old now. I am writing to give you an update about our family.

_____

_____

_____

_____

_____

_____

_____

_____

_____

We will always remember your kindness. We hope you are well.

Sincerely,

_____

3 FOCUS ON WRITING

A VOCABULARY

REVIEW

Complete the sentences with words from the box.

challenge	entertainment	laughter	privacy	siblings
donate	jealous	~~pregnant~~	protect	unique

1. Bobbi McCaughey doesn't want to become _____pregnant_____ again. She thinks eight kids are enough.

2. Some families were _____ when they saw all of the donations the McCaugheys received.

3. The family has some bad days, but they are very happy. There is always a lot of _____ each day.

4. Bobbi and Kenny plan to _____ their kids from the media.

5. Having eight kids is a _____, but Bobbi and Kenny are doing a good job.

6. In a house with ten people, it is difficult to find _____.

7. For _____, the McCaugheys play games, sing songs, and play musical instruments.

8. The septuplets are the same age, but each child is _____. Each has a different personality.

9. Mikayla McCaughey likes all of her _____, but she thinks seven is enough.

10. Today companies do not _____ many things to the McCaughey family.

Read the idioms and expression about families. Then complete the sentences with an idiom or expression about family. Use the correct form of the verb.

an only child: (noun) a person with no siblings

the middle child: (noun) the child with older and younger siblings

sibling rivalry: (noun) competition between brothers and sisters in a family

the black sheep: (noun) the family member who has a different life from the others

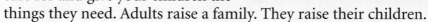

raise a family/children: (verb) care for and give your children the things they need. Adults raise a family. They raise their children.

grow up: (verb) get older. Children grow up to be adults.

take after: (verb) be similar to an older family member, such as a parent or sibling

It runs in the family: (expression) All of the family members have something in common, such as hair color or personality.

1. Everyone in my family went to college. They all work in offices, and they all live in the city. I decided not to go to college. I live on a farm. I love my family, but I am definitely _____.

2. Jane likes to play tennis. She _____ her father. He plays tennis often.

3. Mr. and Mrs. Sullivan were very friendly to their neighbors. Their children are friendly, too. Friendliness _____ Sullivan _____.

4. Patrick and Peter are twins. They are always trying to be better than the other in school and in sports. There is a lot of _____ between them.

5. You need a lot of money to _____. You need to pay for clothes, food, and school.

(continued on next page)

6. Some people think that _____ has more problems than the younger or older siblings.

7. I don't like sharing a bedroom with my little brother. I'm not _____, but sometimes I want to be.

8. Raymond doesn't want to _____. He wants to be a kid forever.

◖ CREATE

Work with a partner. Write six sentences about the McCaughey family. Use the words and phrases from Review and Expand. Put your sentences in time order. Then make a paragraph with your sentences.

_____

_____

_____

_____

_____

_____

B **GRAMMAR:** *Should*

1 *Ian has a fifteen-year-old son, Ken. Ian asks his mother, Ken's grandmother, for advice about giving Ken an allowance (weekly spending money). Read their conversation. Then answer the questions.*

IAN: Mom, should I give Ken an allowance?
MOM: Well, I gave you an allowance when you were Ken's age. So, yes, I think you should.
IAN: Yeah, right, I remember. How much should I give him?
MOM: You shouldn't give him a lot, just enough for small things—a movie with his friends, for example. You should also teach him to save a little "for a rainy day[1]."
IAN: You're right. OK, thanks, Mom.

1. What advice did Ian's mother give him? Make a list on a separate piece of paper. (*Hint:* Look for the word *should* or *shouldn't*.)

2. What form of the verb comes after *should* and *shouldn't*?

---
[1] **for a rainy day:** for a day you need a little extra money

SHOULD	
Should is a helping verb that means "it's a good idea."	$\begin{bmatrix} \text{helping} \\ \text{verb} \end{bmatrix} \begin{bmatrix} \text{main} \\ \text{verb} \end{bmatrix}$ Family members **should eat** dinner together every night. Parents **should speak** with their children often. Children **should talk** to their parents.
For a negative opinion, use **shouldn't**.	Children **shouldn't stay up** too late at night. You **shouldn't listen** to his ideas.
To ask *yes / no* questions, use: **Should + subject + the base form of the verb**	**Should we save** money to buy a new house? **Should teenagers have** part-time jobs?
To ask *wh-* questions, use: **Wh- word + should + subject + the base form of the verb**	**Why should I come** home early? I'm 18 years old! **How much money should I give** to my teenage son?

2 *Some parents have questions for an expert on parenting. Complete the parents' questions and the expert's answers.*

1. PARENT: _____Should parents buy_____ children everything they want?

(parents / buy)

   EXPERT: No, they _____shouldn't_____. They

   _____should_____ teach their children the value of

   money.

2. PARENT: _____ some of the household bills, such as

(my teenage son / pay)
   food and electricity?

   EXPERT: If your teenager has a part-time job, then, yes, he

   _____. But just a small bill to teach him

   about paying bills.

(continued on next page)

3. **PARENT:** _____ my kids play video games?
   (how many hours a day / I / let)

   EXPERT: You _____ let them play video games at

   all. They _____ read books instead.

4. **PARENT:** _____ their children choose a future
   (parents / let)

   career?

   EXPERT: Yes, they _____. Children

   _____ choose a career that they will

   enjoy.

5. **PARENT:** _____ our children clean their bedrooms?
   (we / make)

   EXPERT: No, you _____. Children

   _____ clean their rooms only when they

   want to.

6. **PARENT:** _____ their parents' advice?
   (children / always follow)

   EXPERT: No, they _____. Parents

   _____ let their kids make their own

   decisions.

7. **PARENT:** _____ their kids to do chores, such as
   (parents / require)

   cleaning the bathroom or taking out the garbage?

   EXPERT: Yes, they _____. Your kids

   _____ help out around the house.

8. **PARENT:** When _____ of their parents' house?
   (adult children / move out)

   EXPERT: Adult children _____ move out when

   they can afford a place of their own.

Look at the expert's advice again. Which advice do you agree with? Which do you disagree with?

3 *Read each sentence. Give an opinion with* should *or* shouldn't. *More than one answer is possible. Then share your opinions with a partner.*

1. Alexis shares a bedroom with Natalie and Kelsey. She never has any privacy.

   _____She should . . ._____

2. Bert wants to have 10 children when he grows up.

   _____

3. Bobbi and Kenny's friends helped them a lot after the septuplets were born.

   _____

4. Joel likes to read.

   _____

5. The kids like to play outside.

   _____

6. The neighbors spank[1] their kids.

   _____

C WRITING

In this unit, you read about multiple-birth families.

You are going to **write a paragraph expressing your opinion**. First, interview three classmates and ask their opinions. Ask these questions:
- What is the best number of kids to have in a family? Why?
- What should the mix of children be (if any)? Why?

Then write your opinion. Use the vocabulary and grammar from the unit.*

---

[1] **spank:** hit a child when he or she does something bad

*For Alternative Writing Topics, see page 192. These topics can be used in place of the writing topic for this unit or as homework. The alternative topics relate to the theme of the unit, but may not target the same grammar or rhetorical structures taught in the unit.

In an interview, you ask someone questions to find out information. To learn as much as you can in an interview, ask follow-up questions. A **follow-up question** is a question you ask after you hear the answer to a previous question.

John's question: How many people are there in your family?

Kam's answer: There are thirteen people in my family: my parents and eleven kids. I am the youngest.

John's follow-up question: Wow! What was it like growing up in such a big family?

Kam's answer: My parents had to work very hard to raise all of us. Everyone, even the youngest, had to help to take care of the family. We had to be very patient with each other.

Ask more than one follow-up question, if needed. You can ask a *Yes / No* question or a *Wh-* question. *Wh-* questions usually give more information. Look at these examples:

- Did you enjoy growing up in a big family? (*Yes / No* question)

  Possible Answer: Yes, I did.

- What was it like growing up in such a big family? (*Wh-* question)

  Possible Answer: It was fun. I always had someone to play with. I was never bored.

Other ways to ask a follow-up question:

Can you tell me more about _____?

What else can you tell me about _____?

Is there anything else you want to say about _____?

Ask follow-up questions until you are ready to ask a question about a new topic.

1 *Read each question (Q) and answer (A) on the next page. Then write a follow-up question (F) for each conversation. Write follow-up questions that will give you more information about the person's family. Compare your questions with a partner's.*

1. **Q:** How many kids are there in your family?

    A: Three.

    F: _Are you the oldest?_

2. **Q:** What's the best number of children to have in a family?

    A: I think three is the best number.

    F: _____

3. **Q:** What is the best age range between children in a family?

    A: Four or five years.

    F: _____

4. **Q:** Did you ever want to be an "only child"?

    A: Definitely.

    F: _____

For more about interviewing see Unit 1, *Prepare to Write*, page 19.

2 *Work with a partner. Take turns asking and answering questions.*

QUESTIONS	ANSWERS	POSSIBLE FOLLOW-UP QUESTION	ANSWER
1. How many kids are there in your family?	There are three kids in my family.	What was it like growing up with two siblings?	It was usually fun, but I didn't like sharing my dolls.
2. What's the best number of children in a family?			
3. What's the best age range for kids in a family?			
4. Is it best to have a mix of boys and girls in a family?			

◀ WRITE: An Opinion

In your paragraph, you will express your opinion. You will also give reasons for your opinion. To give an opinion, use the expressions in the chart.

In my opinion, + subject + verb + (the rest of the sentence)	**In my opinion,** families should have a mix of boys and girls.
I think (that) + subject + *should* + main verb + (the rest of the sentence)	**I think that** families **should** have a mix of boys and girls.
I (strongly) believe (that) + subject + *should* + main verb + (the rest of the sentence) **NOTE:** Some people leave out *that*, especially when speaking.	**I (strongly) believe that** families **should** have a mix of boys and girls.

For information about giving reasons, see Unit 2, *Write,* page 38, and Unit 8, *Revise,* page 169.

1 *Read the paragraph. Then answer the questions.*

> In my opinion, I think families should have only one child. I am an only child. I don't have the problems other people have. The people that I interviewed come from "medium-sized" families—families with two or three kids. One reason I think that one child is best is that children are expensive. Parents are worried about money. Can they pay the bills? How will their kids go to college? It's too much. Another reason is that parents are busy. They can't give attention to each child if there are many children. If there is just one child, it is easier for everyone. For all these reasons, I strongly believe that the best number of children in a family is one.

1. What is the writer's opinion?

_____

2. What support does the writer give for his/her opinion?

    a. _____

    b. _____

2 *Write your first draft. Don't worry about the grammar. Just try to make your ideas clear.*

◀ **REVISE:** Writing a Concluding Sentence

A **concluding sentence** is usually the last sentence of a paragraph. A concluding sentence usually repeats or supports the main idea in the topic sentence. Sometimes, the concluding sentence gives an opinion about the main idea or the future.

1 *Read the paragraph. Then read the three concluding sentences. Choose the best one. Explain your choice.*

> I think that families should eat dinner together. One reason is that dinner time is a chance for family members to talk. Everyone is always very busy. But if they sit together at dinner, they can slow down and spend time together. Another reason that I think families should eat together is that it is healthier. If people eat alone or eat fast food, they will become fat and unhealthy. _____
>
> _____

Concluding Sentences:

  a. For these reasons, dinner is my family's favorite meal.

  b. For these reasons, families should have dinner together.

  c. For these reasons, I think eating dinner is very important.

To review topic sentences, see Unit 4, *Write*, page 77.

2 *Write the letter of the concluding sentence next to the topic sentence. Then write what type of concluding sentence it is (repetition, opinion, the future).*

TOPIC SENTENCES	CONCLUDING SENTENCES	TYPES OF CONCLUDING SENTENCES
1. My father has an interesting job.	**a.** He gives us everything we need.	
2. My father has worked hard to be successful.	**b.** I respect him for working so hard.	
3. My father takes good care of our family.	**c.** I want to have a job like my father's.	

3 Look at the first draft of your paragraph. Be sure you have a concluding sentence.

◀ **EDIT: Writing the Final Draft**

Prepare to write the final draft of your paragraph. Check your grammar, spelling, capitalization, and punctuation. Check that you used some of the vocabulary and grammar from the unit. Use the checklist to help you write your final draft. Then neatly write or type your paragraph.

✔ FINAL DRAFT CHECKLIST

- ○ Did you express an opinion?
- ○ Did you use a concluding sentence? Does it support the topic sentence?
- ○ Did you use *should*?
- ○ Did you use vocabulary from the unit?

ALTERNATIVE WRITING TOPICS

Write about one of the topics. Use the vocabulary and grammar from the unit.

1. How does the birth of septuplets (or sextuplets/quintuplets/quadruplets/ triplets) change a family? Think about holidays, birthday parties, vacations, and daily routines such as getting ready in the morning. Write one paragraph about a specific change.

2. Are there any twins or triplets in your family or in a family you know? Write a paragraph about them. How are the children alike? How are they different?

3. Write two paragraphs about someone in your family. In the first paragraph, describe this person today. What does he or she do? Use the simple present tense. In the second paragraph, describe what this person should do in the future, in your opinion. Use the verb *should*.

RESEARCH TOPICS, see page 222.

How Young Is Too Young?

1 FOCUS ON THE TOPIC

A PREDICT

Look at the picture. Discuss the question with the class.

What is happening in the picture?

SHARE INFORMATION

Discuss the questions with a partner.

1. What sports do you like to play or watch? What do you like about them?

2. What are the benefits of being a professional athlete[1]? What are some of the drawbacks?

C
BACKGROUND AND VOCABULARY

1 *Read about three young athletes.*

Most soccer fans say that Brazil's Pelé was the greatest soccer player ever. He showed his **talent** for soccer at a young age. In 1958, when he was just 17 years old, Pelé became the youngest player to win the World Cup with his team. In his career Pelé has had to **deal with** many challenges: being an athlete, being a media star, and being a role model for kids.

In 1997, at the age of 17, Martina Hingis became the youngest #1 women's tennis player. She was a great athlete, but she was not a **mature** woman yet. Martina made some **comments** about other players. For example, in 1998, she called another tennis player "old and slow." Later, her comments were much more **responsible**. When she was 22, Hingis had **difficulties** with her legs and had to stop playing tennis. She started playing again when she was 25 but retired[2] at age 27.

---

[1] **professional athlete:** someone who is paid to play a sport

[2] **retired:** stopped working

Michele Wie became a professional golfer long before she **graduated** from high school. She **earned** over $10 million in her first year. She was 15 years old. Wie is good enough to play professional men's golf. But her **coach** told her that she should continue to play women's golf.

2 *Match the words on the left with the definitions on the right.*

_h_	**1.** talent	**a.** taking care of others and doing what you say you will do
____	**2.** mature	**b.** problems
____	**3.** comments	**c.** received money for doing something
____	**4.** responsible	**d.** grown up, like an adult
____	**5.** difficulties	**e.** finished education at a school
____	**6.** earned	**f.** try to handle a difficulty in the correct way
____	**7.** graduated	**g.** a person who teaches a sport
____	**8.** coach	**h.** natural ability to do something like art, music, or sports
____	**9.** deal with	**i.** ideas a person says or writes about something or someone

A READING ONE: Ready Freddy?

1 *Read the title of the newspaper article. What do you think the title means? Check (✓) your ideas.*

_____ **1.** He is going to change his name.

_____ **2.** He is going to move to another country.

_____ **3.** He is going to become a professional soccer player.

_____ **4.** He is going to go to college.

2 *Read the article.*

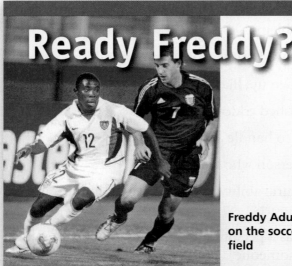

The Metropolitan Herald April 2, 2004

Ready Freddy?

Freddy Adu on the soccer field

by Richard Gray

1 **IN A FEW DAYS**, he will be a professional soccer player. Freddy Adu will **earn** about $500,000 per year. And Nike® will pay him about $1 million to wear their shoes and clothes. That is more than most other U.S. **professional** soccer players earn today. But right now, Adu needs to finish high school.

2 Freddy Adu is 14 years old, and he attends Edison Academic Center. Edison is a school for students with special **talents** in sports or art. Many of them, like Adu, graduate from high school early. At Edison, Adu learns about math, English, history, and, of course, soccer. Adu and the other students also learn how to live in the spotlight[1].

3 There is a whole team of teachers and **coaches** helping Adu to prepare for the professional world. They gave him a job at a preschool[2]. They say that taking care of three-year-olds will teach Adu to be **responsible**. He will need to be responsible in the difficult world of professional sports. His coaches talk to him about the **difficulties** of being famous. For example, sometimes the media say unkind or untrue things about athletes. "People will say that Adu is not **mature**. They will talk about his family. They will say he makes too much money," says one of Adu's coaches. The

[1] **in the spotlight:** famous; seen or watched by the public
[2] **preschool:** a school for children under six years old

coaches help Adu understand that he cannot get angry about these **comments**.

4 At Edison, Adu also gets support from older professional athletes, like Roy Williams from the Dallas Cowboys[3]. Williams told Adu, "Go out and have fun, but take care of yourself." Williams also told him to be careful. He said that people—even your family and friends—can sometimes change when you have a lot of money. "Freddy listens. He asks questions," Williams said.

5 In a few days, life will change forever for Adu. He will graduate from Edison and enter the world of professional soccer. The teachers at Edison think that 14-year-old Adu is mature enough to play pro soccer. But there is no test for maturity[4] at school. The real test will begin after he graduates.

---

[3] **Dallas Cowboys:** a U.S. professional football team
[4] **maturity:** being mature

3 *Look back at your answer to Exercise 1. Was your prediction correct?*

◖ READ FOR MAIN IDEAS

Check (✓) the answer that includes the most important points in the article.

_____ 1. Freddy's teachers and coaches give him advice about the difficulties of being a pro athlete. For example, professional athletes' families sometimes want to take their money.

_____ 2. Freddy Adu will soon become a pro soccer player. He is young, so his teachers and coaches want to prepare him for the professional world. No one thinks he is mature enough.

_____ 3. Freddy Adu is young. But his teachers and coaches are helping him become mature very fast. They are not worried about him going to the professional soccer world.

◖ READ FOR DETAILS

Circle the best answer to complete each statement.

1. Freddy Adu will earn _____ older professional athletes.
   a. less than
   b. the same as
   c. more than

2. Edison is a school for _____.
   a. professional soccer players
   b. soccer and tennis coaches
   c. talented young athletes

3. One difficulty for professional athletes is _____.
   a. taking care of small children
   b. being in the spotlight
   c. taking tests

4. The coaches at Edison are helping Adu learn to _____.
   a. deal with people's comments
   b. earn a lot of money
   c. take care of his family

5. The coaches and teachers at Edison think that Adu is _____.
   a. too young to play professional soccer
   b. strong enough to play for the Dallas Cowboys
   c. ready to become a professional athlete

◖ MAKE INFERENCES

Choose what is most important for each person (or group of people).

People	What Is Most Important?
_____ 1. Freddy Adu	a. to teach Adu about math and other school subjects
_____ 2. Edison teachers	b. to use Adu to earn money
_____ 3. Edison coaches	c. to help Adu understand money
_____ 4. Roy Williams	d. to play soccer
_____ 5. Nike	e. to give good advice on playing soccer
_____ 6. the media	f. to tell everyone if Freddy is not mature

◀ **EXPRESS OPINIONS**

Check (✓) the box that matches your opinion. Then discuss your answers with a partner. Give reasons and ask follow-up questions.

	I AGREE.	IT DEPENDS.	I DISAGREE.
1. Age 14 is too young to become a professional athlete.			
2. You can't learn how to be responsible in school.			
3. $500,000 a year is too much money for a 14-year-old to earn.			

To review giving reasons, see Unit 2, page 38 and Unit 9, page 190. To review asking follow-up questions, see Unit 9, page 188.

1 *Read the imaginary interview with Bram Tarek.*

Bram Tarek:
Young Basketball Star Says "No" to the Pros

Interview by Nicola Quinn

You probably don't know Bram Tarek—not yet. But basketball coaches know him, and they think he has a lot of talent. He is a college basketball star. At 18 years old and after graduating from high school, Bram Tarek is now old enough to join a professional basketball team, but the NBA[1] will have to wait. Tarek wants to graduate from college first.

NQ: Bram, everyone expected you to join the NBA this year. Why did you decide to finish college first?

BT: Well, I planned to join the NBA as soon as I was old enough. But then I met older basketball players. They said I should stay in college.

NQ: Who did you talk to?

BT: Several basketball players. But Kareem Abdul-Jabbar probably helped me the most. He is my biggest basketball hero. He's the greatest. But, in his day, all players had to go to college before joining the NBA. Today it's different. He said college helped the players to become more mature—intellectually and physically.

NQ: But what about the money? How can you say "no" to all that money?

BT: Oh, that was really hard! On the wall in my bedroom, I had photos of all the beautiful cars I wanted to buy!

NQ: So, what happened?

BT: Kareem helped a lot. He really taught me that money is not #1. The important things in life are family, education, and health. And I still have a lot to learn.

NQ: What exactly do you need to learn?

BT: I need to learn more about working with other people—especially with people I don't agree with. I want to be a leader like Kareem. Thirty years from now, I want people to say "Bram Tarek was—or is—a great athlete, a great leader, and a good person," not "Bram Tarek was a great athlete with a lot of expensive cars when he was 18."

[1] **NBA:** National Basketball Association. All professional basketball teams in the U.S. are in the NBA.

2 Write **T** (true) or **F** (false). Discuss your answers with a partner.

_____ **1.** Bram Tarek wants to finish college before he plays pro basketball.

_____ **2.** Kareem Abdul-Jabbar thinks that college is very important.

_____ **3.** Kareem Abdul-Jabbar thinks that money makes athletes happy.

_____ **4.** Bram Tarek wanted to buy lots of cars, but now he thinks cars are less important than his education.

_____ **5.** Tarek wants people to think that he is a good person.

C INTEGRATE READINGS ONE AND TWO

◀ STEP 1: Organize

Work with a partner. Fill in the information from each reading in the chart.

	FREDDY ADU	BRAM TAREK
1. What is he learning before he joins the professional world?	Adu . . .	Tarek . . .
2. Where or how is he learning these lessons?		
3. What are some difficulties that young pro players might have?		

A TV reporter is interviewing Coach Williams from the University of Eastern Nebraska and Coach Hay from Edison High School. Complete the interview with information from Organize.

Coach Williams and Coach Hay, thank you for being here. Tell us about the difficulties for a young player who goes pro.

1. Well, _____

_____

2. That's right. But also, _____

_____

So players need to learn more than a sport to go pro . . .

3. Yes, they need to learn _____

_____

4. I agree. They also need to _____

_____

And where can they learn these things?

5. They need to go _____

_____

6. _____

_____

3 FOCUS ON WRITING

A VOCABULARY

◖ REVIEW

Cross out one word, phrase, or sentence in each item that does not make sense.

1. Joe was a really good (~~cooking~~ / running / basketball) **coach.**

2. I think that Kelly **earns** (*a good job* / *good grades in school* / *a lot of money*).

3. The girl who takes care of our children is only 15, but she is **mature.** (*She knows what to do in an emergency.* / *She stays calm if the kids are angry.* / *She talks to her boyfriend on the phone while she babysits.*)

4. I want to have a big party after I **graduate** from (*the supermarket* / *college* / *high school*).

5. Jennifer is a very **responsible** worker. When you ask her to do something, she (*forgets* / *does it well* / *makes sure the job is finished*).

6. Aisha has great **talent** for (*singing* / *walking* / *tennis*).

7. After I graduated from high school, my family **expected** me to (*go to college* / *get a job* / *do my homework*).

8. Pelé is one of my **heroes.** (*He was a good dancer.* / *He was a great athlete.* / *He was a good role model for kids.*)

9. Scott had some **difficulties** after he became a pro basketball player. (*He didn't know how to deal with the media.* / *He hurt his arm and couldn't play any more.* / *He made millions of dollars.*)

10. Scott also didn't know how to **deal with** the media. (*He got angry with their questions.* / *He played basketball every day.* / *He got upset about their comments about him.*)

These idioms come from sports, but they can be used in everyday life.

1 *Study the sports idioms. There is one example from sports and another from everyday school life.*

hog the (ball): *keep the (ball) to yourself, control use of something, not share (something) with your group or teammates*

Mary doesn't hog the ball. She passes the ball to her teammates when necessary.

Mary doesn't hog the paint in art class. She shares with other students.

call the shots: *make all the decisions for a group*

Listen to the coach. He calls all the shots.

Bill is our class president. He calls all the shots on the student council.

get the ball rolling: *start something, like a conversation between people*

Let's get the ball rolling, team. Go out on the field and win this game!

Let's get the ball rolling, class. First, let's talk about last night's homework.

be / get on the ball: *be / become intelligent, focused, ready to act*

On the tennis court, Vincent is always on the ball. He thinks only about the match.

Vincent! Wake up. Get on the ball! Pay attention! We are on page 204.

be a team player: *work well with other people on a team or group members, cooperate with other people*

If you want to play on this team, you have to be a team player. Don't hog the ball and don't try to be a star.

If you want an "A" on your group project in this class, you have to be a team player.

2 *Match the situations with the correct responses.*

Situations

1. Bryan always listens carefully and thinks about his group's opinions. You can say: _____

2. You are working with a group of classmates. Your assignment is to discuss why Freddy Adu should or should not turn pro. You are the group leader. To begin, you say: _____

3. You want to try to score a goal, but your teammate does not pass the ball to you or anyone. You say to your teammate: _____

4. You forgot your mother's birthday, but your secretary remembered. She sent your mother some flowers. You say: _____

5. You are the captain of the soccer team, and one of your teammates isn't listening to your instruction. You tell him: _____

Responses

a. "Hey, Jimmy. Don't hog the ball!"

b. "He's a real team player."

c. "Thanks for doing that for me, Dana. You are always on the ball."

d. "OK, who wants to get the ball rolling? Debbie, how about you?"

e. "I call all the shots during the game."

1 *Interview a classmate, teacher, or coach. Ask this person five questions. Use some of the words from the box.*

coach	expected	mature
deal with	graduate	responsible
difficulties	heroes	talent
earns[1]		

1. _____

2. _____

3. _____

4. _____

5. _____

Write the person's answers.

1. _____

2. _____

3. _____

4. _____

5. _____

On a separate piece of paper, write a paragraph about the person you interviewed.

---

[1] We usually do not ask how much money a person earns at his or her job.

2 *Study the pictures. What are the people saying? Write their words on the line.*
Use the vocabulary from Expand.

Teacher: _____

Student: _____   Student: _____

Compare your answers with a partner's. Explain your choices.

1 *Read each statement. Then choose the sentence that represents the meaning of the statement.*

1. Some people think Adu is **very mature** for his age.
   a. Adu is less mature than other kids his age.
   b. Adu is more mature than other kids his age.

2. Adu is **too young** to play pro soccer in England.
   a. At his age, Adu can't play pro soccer in England.
   b. At his age, Adu can play pro soccer in England.

3. Kareem Abdul-Jabbar is **too old** to play with the NBA.
   a. Abdul-Jabbar can't play with the NBA.
   b. Abdul-Jabbar can play with the NBA.

4. Kareem Abdul-Jabbar is not **too old** to teach younger players.
   a. Abdul-Jabbar can't teach younger players.
   b. Abdul-Jabbar can teach younger players.

5. The teachers think Adu is **mature enough** to play professional soccer.
   a. They think it's not OK for him to play professional soccer.
   b. They think it's OK for him to play professional soccer.

6. Bram Tarek is **old enough** to join the NBA.
   a. At his age, Tarek can't play in the NBA.
   b. At his age, Tarek can play in the NBA

7. Many people think that Adu is not **mature enough** to turn pro.
   a. They think it's not OK for Adu to turn pro at his age.
   b. They think it's OK for Adu to turn pro at his age.

VERY, TOO, AND ENOUGH

Use **very** before an adjective to make the adjective stronger.	[adjective] That car is **very expensive**. I'm not sure if I should spend so much.
Use **too** before an adjective to show a problem.	[adjective] That car is **too expensive** for me to buy. I'll buy a less expensive one.
Use **enough** after an adjective or before a noun. Use *enough* to say something about "amount."	[adjective] The gray car isn't **cheap enough** for me to buy. I think I'll buy the yellow one. [noun] I have **enough money** to buy the yellow car, [noun] but I don't have **enough money** to buy the gray one. I'll buy the yellow one.

These sentences mean the same thing:
   The gray car is **too expensive** for me to buy.
   I don't have **enough money** to buy the gray car.

These sentences also mean the same thing:
   The yellow car isn't **too expensive**.
   I have **enough money** to buy the yellow one.

2 *Put the words in order to make sentences.*

1. Kareem Abdul-Jabbar / basketball / too / is / play / to / old / pro

    _____

2. a / is / Joe / musician / talented / very

    _____

3. basketball / tall / to / is / play / enough / Kevin

    _____

4. enough / drive / not / is / Jamie / old / to

    _____

5. pick up / Sally / not / is / strong / enough / to / the box

    _____

6. Martina / win / at / Wimbledon / enough / was / to / good

    _____

3 *Study the picture. Finish the sentences with the words provided. For the last two, write your own sentence about Ayala. Use **too** or **enough**.*

1. Jeff / short _Jeff is too short to ride The Sled._____

2. Jeff / young _____

3. Jeff / heavy _____

4. Charlie / tall _____

5. Charlie / heavy _____

6. Charlie / old _____

7. Ayala _____

8. Ayala _____

4 *Answer the questions with **too** or **enough**.*

1. What are some things that you are too old to do now?

_____

_____

2. What are some things that you are not old enough to do yet?

_____

_____

C WRITING

In this unit, you read about two very young athletes. Read the letter from a parent to an online advice group.

You are going to **write a response giving advice** to Diana. Use the vocabulary and grammar from the unit.*

http://www.adviceforyoungatheletes.com/contact

My daughter is 12 years old. She loves sports and she has a lot of talent. Every year, coaches call us to ask her to be on their teams. Now, professional coaches are calling because they want her to get ready for the professional teams. I know that some young athletes go pro at 14. I want her to do what she loves, but I am worried that she is too young to think about becoming a professional. What age is old enough to become a pro athlete?

—*Diana*, San Rafael, CA, USA

---

*For Alternative Writing Topics, see page 217. These topics can be used in place of the writing topic for this unit or as homework. The alternative topics relate to the theme of the unit, but may not target the same grammar or rhetorical structures taught in the unit.

◖ **PREPARE TO WRITE: Brainstorming**

To help you plan your paragraph, you are going to **brainstorm** as a prewriting activity. To review brainstorming, see Unit 2, page 37.

Work with a partner. Make a list of the pros and cons of becoming a pro athlete at a young age. Think about Freddy Adu and Bram Tarek. Add your own ideas. Write the benefits in the (+) column and the drawbacks in the (−) column.

+	−

Look at the two columns. What's your opinion? What will you tell Diana?

◖ **WRITE: A Letter of Advice**

When you give advice you need to think about your audience. Who will receive your advice? Follow the steps.

Steps in Giving Advice

1. Show that you understand the problem.

2. Give your advice.

3. Give a reason for your advice.

4. Conclude by offering help or a final comment.

1 *Read Danny's letter to the online advice group.*

○○○

◄ ► | ⌂ | C | + | http://www.adviceforyoungatheletes.com/contact | ▾ | | ⊙

Dear Group,
I'm 15 years old and I love playing on the tennis and baseball teams at school. I have to practice every day after school. I don't have enough time to finish my homework. My grades are falling, and I'm always tired. I don't want to give up my sports because I love them both. I also want to try to get an athletic scholarship to pay for college. What should I do?
Danny, *Perth, Australia*

2 *Read the sentences. Then put the sentences in order. Answers may vary. Compare your answers with a partner's.*

_____ This is a good idea if you want to get an athletic scholarship to pay for college.

_____ I think you should choose one sport.

_2_ I played sports when I was in high school, too.

_____ If you do this, you will have more time for school work.

_1_ I understand your situation.

_____ You will also need enough time to sleep. Your body needs time to rest.

_____ Colleges will also notice your grades.

_____ I'm sure you will make the right decision.

_____ Good luck.

_3_ I was often too tired at night to finish my homework or even eat dinner!

_____ If you focus on one sport, you will get better at it. Colleges will notice.

_____ You'll also have more time for homework.

3 Write a letter to Danny using the sentences in Exercise 2. Follow the steps in giving advice. Then compare your advice with a partner's.

Dear Danny,

_____

_____

_____

_____

_____

_____

_____

_____

_____

_____

_____

_____

_____

_____

_____

_____

_____

_____

To review *should*, see Unit 9, page 185.

4 *Write the first draft of your answer to Diana.*

◀ **REVISE: Giving Strong Advice**

When people have a problem, they ask for advice. If the problem is very serious, then the advice needs to be stronger. Look at the graph.

casual advice	specific advice	stronger advice	the strongest advice
There are a couple of choices.	This is a good choice.	Choose this. If you don't, there might be a negative result.	There is no other choice.

Casual Advice When giving someone choices, use *can and might* **+ the base form of the verb**.	You **can** watch one TV show now and study for your test later. You **might** watch TV for a little while and then study for your test after that. *Can* and *might* mean the same thing in these sentences. Do not use *can't* or *might not* to give advice.
Specific Advice When giving someone a specific piece of advice, use *should or ought to* **+ the base form of the verb**.	You **should study** for the test. (I think it is a good idea for you to do it.) You **shouldn't** watch TV. You **ought to study** for the test. Do not use *ought to* in a negative sentence. ~~You **ought not** to watch TV.~~
Stronger Advice When you think there is only one choice, use *had better* **+ the base form of the verb**. *Had better* also suggests that there will be a negative result if the person does not do the right thing. *Had better* is present tense. The form doesn't change.	[strong advice] You **had better study** for the test, [negative result] or you might fail the course! I **had better study** tonight. He **had better study** tonight, too. We **had better not watch** TV all night.
The Strongest Advice When you think there is no choice, use *have to* **+ the base form of the verb**.	You **have to study**. This is a very important test! Do not use *don't have to* to give advice. You use *don't have to* to say that something is not necessary.

1 *Jack has many problems at work. Read his problems. Then give him one piece of advice for each problem. Use* **can, might, should, shouldn't, ought to, had better (not)**, *or* **have to**. *Answers may vary. Compare your answers with a partner's and say whose advice is stronger.*

1. I don't like my job. _____

_____

2. I haven't had a vacation in three years. _____

_____

3. I don't know what to do with my time when I'm not at work. _____

_____

4. I don't make enough money to pay my rent. _____

_____

5. I never see my family because I'm at work all the time. _____

_____

6. I work twelve hours a day. _____

_____

7. I always arrive late for work. _____

_____

8. My boss always asks me to work late. _____

_____

9. My office is too small. _____

_____

10. My job is so stressful I have a stomach problem. _____

_____

11. My job isn't exciting anymore. _____

_____

12. I share a desk with five people. _____

_____

2 *Now look at your answer to Diana. Underline the advice you give. Is it strong enough? Is it too strong? Make changes as needed.*

◀ **EDIT:** Writing the Final Draft

Prepare to write the final draft of your letter. Check your grammar, spelling, capitalization, and punctuation. Check that you used some of the vocabulary and grammar from the unit. Use the checklist to help you write your final draft. Then neatly write or type your letter.

✔ FINAL DRAFT CHECKLIST

- ○ Did you give advice to Diana?
- ○ Is your advice the right strength?
- ○ Did you use *very, too,* and *enough*?
- ○ Did you use vocabulary from this unit?

ALTERNATIVE WRITING TOPICS

Write about one of the topics. Use the vocabulary and grammar from the unit.

1. What are some of the difficulties for professional athletes?

2. Sometimes professional athletes do or say things that are irresponsible. Write about a professional athlete who did something that was irresponsible or immature. Why do you think he or she did it?

3. Write about a person who did something important at a young age. How did this person's life change as a result?

RESEARCH TOPICS, see page 223.

RESEARCH TOPICS

UNIT 1: The Friendship Page

(RESEARCH

A **tribute** is something good that you say or write about a special person.

Learn about the Tributes page and write a tribute.

Step 1: Go to The Friendship Page. Look at the Tributes page.

Step 2: Read some of the tributes on the Tributes page.

Step 3: Write a tribute about one of your friends or a family member.

Step 4: Give the tribute to that person.

UNIT 2: What Will I Wear?

(RESEARCH

Interview people about their uniforms.

Step 1: Speak with two people who wear different uniforms, for example, a police officer or a nurse. Ask the following questions. Be sure to ask follow-up questions (questions about their answers).

	1. _____	2. _____
Why do you wear a uniform? (What is your job?)		
What do you wear? Describe the parts of your uniform.		
Do you like your uniform? Why or why not?		
Other questions:		

Step 2: Look at the information you collected from the two people. Answer these questions:

What was the same?

What was different?

Which uniform do you like more? Why?

Step 3: Report back to the class.

UNIT 3: Art for Everyone

◖ RESEARCH

These are some artists that Keith Haring knew well. Choose one artist from the list.

Cindy Sherman

Roy Lichtenstein

Claes Oldenburg

Robert Rauschenberg

Jean-Michel Basquiat

Step 1: Learn about this artist. Write five to ten sentences about this artist. What is important to know about this artist?

Step 2: Find one piece of art by this artist. Then write five to ten sentences about the piece of art. Answer some of these questions:

What do you see in the art?

Do you like this piece of art?

How does it make you feel?

Step 3: Share your writing and the piece of art with a partner. Read your partner's sentences and look at the piece of art. Take notes.

Artist's name: _____

What do you know about this artist?

What do you know about this artist's art?

UNIT 4: What's It Worth to You?

◀ RESEARCH

A **thrift shop** is a store that sells "secondhand" clothes, furniture, and other old things at a cheap price. Everything at a thrift shop is secondhand—it was owned by another person before. An **antiques store** also has secondhand items, but the things at antiques stores are rarer and more expensive.

Visit a thrift shop or an antiques store. Then follow these steps.

Step 1: Choose one item in the store. Learn about the item. Take a photograph if possible. Then write answers to these questions:

What is it?

How old is it?

What does it look like?

Is it valuable? Why or why not?

Step 2: Write a paragraph about the item. Use some of your answers to the questions above. Start your paragraph like this: *"I learned about an interesting item in a thrift shop / antiques store."*

Step 3: Share your writing and photograph with a partner. Read your partner's paragraph. Then answer these questions:

Did the writer indent the first line of the paragraph?

Did the writer use margins correctly?

Which sentences explain why the item is interesting? Underline them.

UNIT 5: Strength in Numbers

◀ RESEARCH

Search the Internet for other organizations that help teenagers. Notice how the organizations market themselves: Do they use a lot of pictures? Do they have special activities? Do they use words or expressions that teens like? Do they talk about important issues for teens?

Imagine you work for the Guardian Angels in your city or town. Design and write an advertisement for the Urban Angels. Use words and pictures to get young people to join the Urban Angels program in your community.

UNIT 6: Going Out of Business?

◖ RESEARCH

Interview the owner or an employee of a family-owned business.

Step 1: Write down the answers to these questions. Think of your own questions, too.

1. What is the name of the business?

2. What kind of business is it?

3. Is it a small business or a large business?

4. When did it open?

5. Is it a successful business? Tell me why or why not.

6. Is there any competition with other businesses? Which ones?

7. Do you like working here? Tell me why or why not.

8. Your questions:_____

Step 2: Write one paragraph about this business. Use the information you collected.

UNIT 7: Flying High and Low

◖ RESEARCH

Think of a famous person who is not living today. Collect information about this person and pictures, if possible.

Step 1: Look in the library and on the Internet for information about this person.

Step 2: Make a timeline of this person's life like the timeline on page 138. Write the important dates in the "Dates" column. Then write a sentence about each date in the "What happened?" column. Include the good times and bad times in this person's life.

Step 3: Write a paragraph about this person. Use simple past tense verbs when you write about past events. Also, use time order words and expressions. Begin your paragraph with the sentence: "_____ [name] had a(n) _____ [adj., such as interesting] life."

UNIT 8: Are We There Yet?

◖ RESEARCH

Most cities have traffic problems. How does your city or town control traffic? Find out more about traffic in your city.

Step 1: Choose a traffic problem in your city or town. To find information, look on the Internet, talk to a police officer, or call the traffic department.

Step 2: Think of a possible solution. Take notes. What are the advantages and disadvantages of this solution?

Step 3: Write a paragraph about the problem and your possible solution. Begin your paragraph like this: "_____ *[name of your city] tries to control its traffic problems. For example, . . . "*

UNIT 9: Full House

◖ RESEARCH

How much does it cost to raise a child?

Step 1: Imagine that you are the proud parent of a 10-year-old boy or girl. Complete the chart. Find out how much the items cost for one child for one year. Look on the Internet and visit stores. Add more items to the list. Then calculate the amount for the eight McCaughey children.

SUMMARY REPORT		
Expenses for one year	**For one child**	**For the eight McCaughey children**
Haircut		
Visit to the doctor		
Lessons (piano, dance, karate, etc.)		
One pair of shoes		

SUMMARY REPORT

Expenses for one year	For one child	For the eight McCaughey children
Clothes (shirts, pants, dresses, underwear, pajamas, etc.)		
Computer game		
Toy or book		
Movie or video rental		
Other: _____		
_____		
_____		
Total:		

Step 2: Write a paragraph about how much it costs to raise children. Begin your paragraph like this: *"Having children is expensive because . . ."*

Step 3: Share your summary report with the class.

UNIT 10: How Young Is Too Young?

◖ RESEARCH

Work in groups and find out more about Freddy Adu or another professional sports star. Make a timeline of the important events in his or her life so far.

Step 1: With your group, decide whom to research—Freddy Adu or another athlete.

(continued on next page)

Step 2: Divide the research. Here are two ways to do it:

- If you can search the Internet, divide up the research as follows. One person researches each of the following sites:

    1. Major League Soccer (MLS) websites (for Freddy Adu or another soccer player)

    2. Sports TV sites (ESPN)

    3. major newspaper sites (*New York Times, Washington Post*)

- If you can go to the library, ask a librarian for help to find articles in:

    1. sports magazines

    2. newspapers

    3. other magazines

Step 3: Bring all of your information to your group and fill in a timeline for the life of your sports star. (*Hint:* Read the titles. Titles give important information about the articles.)

Step 4: Share your timeline with the class.

GRAMMAR BOOK REFERENCES

NorthStar: Reading and Writing Level 1, Second Edition	Focus on Grammar Level 1, Second Edition	Azar's Basic English Grammar, Third Edition
Unit 1 Questions with *Be* and *Have*	**Unit 5** The Present of *Be: Yes / No* Questions, Questions with *Who* and *What* **Unit 6** The Present of *Be:* Questions with *Where*; Prepositions of Place **Unit 12** The Simple Present: *Be* and *Have*	**Chapter 2** Using *Be* and *Have*
Unit 2 The Future with *Will*		**Chapter 10** Future Time: Using *Will*: 10-6
Unit 3 Simple Past of *Be* and *Have*	**Part III** The Verb *Be:* Past **Unit 22** The Simple Past: Regular and Irregular Verbs; *Yes / No* Questions	**Chapter 8** Expressing Past Time, Part 1
Unit 4 The Simple Present	**Part IV** The Simple Present	**Chapter 3** Using the Simple Present
Unit 5 Pronouns and Possessive Adjectives	**Unit 2** *This is / These are*; Subject Pronouns **Unit 4** *That is / Those are*; Possessive Adjectives; Plural Nouns **Unit 24** Subject and Object Pronouns	**Chapter 2** Using *My, Your, His, Her, Our, Their*: 2-5 **Chapter 6** Subject Pronouns and Object Pronouns: 6-3

GRAMMAR BOOK REFERENCES

NorthStar: Reading and Writing Level 1, Second Edition	*Focus on Grammar Level 1,* Second Edition	Azar's *Basic English Grammar,* Third Edition
Unit 6 *There is / There are*	**Unit 26** *There is / There are*	**Chapter 5** *There + Be:* 5-4 *There + Be: Yes / No* Questions: 5-5
Unit 7 The Simple Past	**Part VII** The Simple Past	**Chapter 8** Expressing Past Time, Part 1 **Chapter 9** Expressing Past Time, Part 2
Unit 8 Comparative Adjectives	**Unit 28** Comparative Adjectives	**Chapter 16** Making Comparisons
Unit 9 *Should*		**Chapter 13** Using *Should:* 13-1
Unit 10 *Very, Too,* and *Enough*		**Chapter 12** Using *Very* and *Too* + Adjective: 12-7

CREDITS

Photo Credits: Page 1 (left) Shutterstock, (middle) Shutterstock, (right) Shutterstock; **Page 5** (top) Bronwyn Polson, (bottom) www.friendship.com.au; **Page 8** (left) Photos.com/Jupiterimages, (right) Photos.com/Jupiterimages; **Page 14** www.friendship.com.au; **Page 25** (top) DAJ/Getty Images, (bottom) Moodboard/Corbis; **Page 26** (left) DAJ/Getty Images, (right) VStock LLC/age fotostock; **Page 27** (left) Marcus Mok/Getty Images, (right) David Davis/Fotolia.com; **Page 43** © 1981 Muna Tseng Dance Projects, Inc. New York; **Page 44** (left) © The Estate of Keith Haring, (right) © The Estate of Keith Haring; **Page 45** (top) © The Estate of Keith Haring, (bottom) Shutterstock; **Page 46** (top) Gianni Dagli Orti/Corbis, (bottom) Arte & Immagini srl/Corbis; **Page 47** Bernard Gotfryd/Getty Images; **Page 51** (left) © The Estate of Keith Haring, (right) © The Estate of Keith Haring; **Page 67** Iofoto/Dreamstime.com; **Page 68** (top) Iofoto/Dreamstime.com, (bottom left) John Sommers II/Reuters/Corbis, (bottom right) Guy Motil/Corbis; **Page 83** Brad Guice; **Page 84** The Alliance of the Guardian Angels; **Page 85** The Alliance of the Guardian Angels; **Page 87** The Alliance of the Guardian Angels; **Page 88** The Alliance of the Guardian Angels; **Page 90** The Alliance of the Guardian Angels; **Page 93** DAREarts Foundation Inc. for Children; **Page 94** John Labbe/Getty Images; **Page 98** The Alliance of the Guardian Angels; **Page 109** Shutterstock; **Page 111** Stockbyte/Getty Images; **Page 118** Warner Bros./Photofest; **Page 135** Bettmann/Corbis; **Page 140** Bettmann/Corbis; **Page 151** Color Day Production/Getty Images; **Page 159** Robert Brenner/PhotoEdit; **Page 161** Stephen Studd/Getty Images; **Page 165** (left) Ian Klein/iStockphoto.com, (right) Shutterstock; **Page 171** Courtesy of the author; **Page 175** (top) Dana Fineman/Copyright 1998/Corbis Sygma, (bottom) Shutterstock; **Page 176** Time Life Pictures/Getty Images; **Page 178** (top) Bettmann/Corbis, (bottom) Taro Yamasaki/Getty Images; **Page 194** (top) George Tiedemann/GT Images/Corbis, (bottom) Peter Parks/Getty Images; **Page 195** David Bergman/Corbis; **Page 196** Karim Jaafar/Getty Images; **Page 199** Shutterstock; **Page 200** Larry Williams/Larry Williams and Associates/Corbis.

Illustration Credits: Aphik Diseño, **Pages 71, 209;** Paul Hampson, **Pages 207, 210;** Derek Mueller, **Pages 34, 35, 45, 65, 193;** Dusan Petriçic, **Page 183;** Gary Torrisi, **Pages 107, 125, 128, 131, 134, 154, 202;** Deborah White, **Page 78.**

Notes

H.w Review unit 1 for test monday.

P.s 25, 26, 27, 28   Homework

7/10/2014 → P 29 and a, P 30

Notes

Notes

Notes

Notes

Notes

Notes